OASIS OR MIRAGE?
WHICH JESUS ARE YOU FOLLOWING?

BY
TERRA KERN

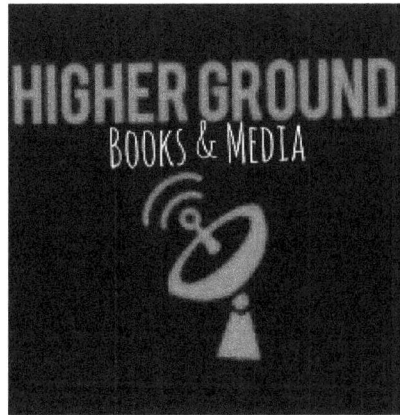

Higher Ground Books & Media
Springfield, Ohio.
http://highergroundbooksandmedia.com

Printed in the United States of America 2021

OASIS OR MIRAGE?
WHICH JESUS ARE YOU FOLLOWING?

BY
TERRA KERN

FOREWORD

Over 22 years as a minister at Mt Zion in Clarkston, I have
worked directly with many people and met even more. In late
2018/early 2019, I met Brandon Kern and his wife Alexis.
Immediately, I was drawn to work with this couple as he was
taking steps to get more fully established in his childhood
faith and his wife was wanting more in the Lord. During the
summer of 2019, they completed a Discipleship group we host
at our home on Sunday evenings. Around that time, I began to
connect with Brandon's mother—Terra Kern.

Terra was also a new member to the church, and she too
wanted to get involved in a Discipleship group. Shortly
thereafter, she asked if I would read some of her writings as
she was preparing a new book. Little did I know *Forgiven and
Not Forgotten* was coming forth and being woven into a
compelling story of Terra's life, the pain and the triumphs,
and a true demonstration of the depth of Christ's love for all
mankind. Her genuine communication, her openness and
honesty, and use of revelation through the Word, is very
impactful. Each page led to the next, becoming chapters, and
ultimately a book!

In her latest book, *OASIS OR MIRAGE: WHICH JESUS ARE
YOU FOLLOWING?* we are confronted with a question that
must be answered. From Terra's accepted definition of an
oasis, Jesus is offering His followers a fertile place to grow and
be life for others. At the heart of the book, Jesus is calling His
church to walk in maturity and demonstrate the fruit of the
kingdom. While the mirage is offering similar looking things,
they only come to enslave us to lies brought forth by darkness
masquerading as light. Terra sets a foundation for the Oasis
available to us in Jesus Christ through strong use of the Word
of God, so we can contrast it against the mirages all around us.
I thoroughly enjoyed the chapters about fruitfulness and her
ability to provide example after example demonstrating her

thought-provoking stance. Terra has a sincere desire to introduce everyone to the Jesus she met as a little girl, the same Jesus who met her and her family again and again over the years and brought them to the place where they thrive in Him.

Ezekiel 47:12 shares imagery of us, the people of God, rooted and grounded as the trees of righteousness providing food and medicine, bearing our fruit in every season. OASIS OR MIRAGE takes us on a journey to be a fruitful demonstration of the King! I have always seen the Word of the God as an encourager to help us take a step higher and to keep us moving forward in His call— "pressing towards the prize of the upward call." Let this book be an encouragement to you and the unfolding story of your life He has been writing, even before you knew the Author, to share your story every day like Terra so freely shares hers.

Richard Nowik, Associate Pastor
Mt Zion
Clarkston, MI

PREFACE

The Holy Spirit put a grieving within my own spirit that led me to cry out and seek Him as to why. As I sought Him, He revealed to me that He wanted me to write another book. So, I began to pray and press in further to receive what He wanted me to write about.

He reminded me of the following Scriptures from the book of John. John1:1-4 "In the beginning was the Word, and the Word was with God, and the Word was God. He was in the beginning with God. All things were made through Him, and without Him nothing was made that was made. In Him was life, and the life was the light of men."

And also of John 1:14 "And the Word became flesh and dwelt among us, and we beheld His glory, the glory as of the only begotten of the Father, full of grace and truth."

Next, He brought back to my memory John the Baptist testifying of Jesus in John 1:29-34, The next day John saw Jesus coming toward him, and said, "Behold! The Lamb of God who takes away the sin of the world! This is He of whom I said, 'After me comes a Man who is preferred before me, for He was before me.' I did not know Him; but that He should be revealed to Israel, therefore I came baptizing with water." And John bore witness, saying, "I saw the Spirit descending from heaven like a dove, and He remained upon Him. I did not know Him, but He who sent me to baptize with water said to me, 'Upon whom you see the Spirit descending and remaining on Him, this is He who baptizes with the Holy Spirit.' And I have seen and testified that this is the Son of God."

In refreshing my memory, the Holy Spirit reminded me that the Word is fully Jesus. The whole Word, every word in the Word is Jesus. Therefore, if any word or part is left out, it is not fully Jesus, or in other words, a different Jesus. And unfortunately, there are a variety of different "Jesuses" being followed out in the world today.

When the Holy Spirit revealed this to me, I sensed His deep sorrow within my own spirit and felt heartbroken. I wanted to please Him and write the book. But at that point, I only had a concept of the theme of the book. I couldn't even put it into words other than the cheesy question of, "Will the real Jesus please stand up?" I knew that wasn't what the book would be called at all, but rather was the concept of it. Then finally after days of pondering over this, the Holy Spirit spoke and asked, "Who is being followed, Jesus the oasis or Jesus the mirage?" I knew right then and there how to proceed. As my oldest daughter likes to say, "The Holy Spirit is a genius!"

The explanations and comparisons of an oasis and a mirage are the basis of this book. Throughout, you will find this book to be rich in Scripture, and it must be, for Jesus is the entire Word of God.

2 Timothy 2:15-17 "Be diligent to present yourself approved to God, a worker who does not need to be ashamed, rightly dividing the word of truth. But shun profane and idle babbling, for they will increase to more ungodliness. And their message will spread like cancer…"

Matthew 7:21-23 "Not everyone who says to Me, 'Lord, Lord,' shall enter the kingdom of heaven, but he who does the will of My Father in heaven. Many will say to Me in that day, 'Lord, Lord, have we not prophesied in Your name, cast out demons in Your name, and done many wonders in Your name?' And I will declare to them, 'I never knew you; depart from Me, you who practice lawlessness!'"

Ephesians 5:26-27 that He might sanctify and cleanse her with the washing of water by the word, that He might present her Himself a glorious church, not having spot or wrinkle or any such thing, but that she should be holy and without blemish.

Revelation 22:14-15 Blessed are those who do His commandments, that they may have the right to the tree of life and may enter through the gates into the city. But outside are the dogs and sorcerers and sexually immoral and murderers and idolaters, and whoever loves and practices a lie.

It is my prayer that as you read the pages of this book, you understand that the Holy Spirit is revealing the Truth, the True Jesus, Jesus the oasis, helping us to rightly divide the word of truth. Not to point fingers or bring criticism or condemnation, but rather, in the hopes that through Him, the world might be saved from condemnation, for without Him we are already condemned.

John 3:17-19 "For God did not send His Son into the world to condemn the world, but that the world through Him might be saved. He who believes in Him is not condemned; but he who does not believe is condemned already, because he has not believed in the name of the only begotten Son of God. And this is the condemnation, that the light has come into the world, and men loved darkness rather than light, because their deeds were evil."

CHAPTER ONE

OASIS VERSUS MIRAGE

When the Holy Spirit spoke and gave me the premise of this book as being Jesus the oasis or Jesus the mirage, of course the first thing I did was to look into both, and what I discovered was astounding. From there, the revelations kept coming in. I praise and thank Him for those revelations as it became plain that His desire for all to know the real Jesus is born from nothing but pure and unadulterated love for us all, for every single person born from the least to the greatest. And that His deep desire is that not one person should ever perish. So, with that being said, let's see what He has been revealing.

The definition and explanation of an oasis are as follows: an oasis is a fertile place where there is life that is fed from water in the midst of deserts or dry places. It's a fertile island of life in the ocean of extremely hot temperatures of the desert and is formed by ever flowing rivers of water beneath the surface of the desert, creating a spring fed pool of water at its center. Every once in a while, it does rain in the desert which in turn feeds the streams and rivers that sustain the oasis. Without the water, an oasis cannot survive. An oasis is not only a fertile island of life, but also gives, supports, and sustains life to all that have been dwelling in or traveling through the desert or dry places.

On the other hand, the definition and explanation of a mirage is an optical illusion or phenomenon in which the image of a distinct object, like an oasis, is made to appear nearby where there is light refracted through a layer of hot air on the desert floor. Or an object, like an oasis, that seems to be just ahead but doesn't really exist. It's a reflection of light passing through hot air that can trick the mind into interpreting and therefore believing the sight is something real. What is important to note and will be further discussed in depth within this book, is that refraction is the "bending of light" through "hot air". In colloquial speech, or in other words, in conversational language, the phrase "hot air" is defined as lies, exaggerations, and nonsense.

Now that we have explored what an oasis is and what a mirage is, we need to understand whom and what Jesus is. First, as touched on in the preface, we must understand that Jesus is the entire Word of God, and we learn this in the first book of John. John1:1-4 "In the beginning was the Word, and the Word was with God, and the Word was God. He was in the beginning with God. All things were made through Him, and without Him nothing was made that was made. In Him was life, and the life was the light of men." And also in John 1:14 "And the Word became flesh and dwelt among us, and we beheld His glory, the glory as of the only begotten of the Father, full of grace and truth." And in Revelation 19:13 "He was clothed with a robe dipped in blood, and His name is called The Word of God."

Also in Matthew 4:4 …" It is written that man shall not live by bread alone, but by every word that proceeds from the mouth of God." Here Jesus is quoting Deuteronomy 8:3 where Moses said "So he humbled you, allowed you to hunger, and fed you with manna which you did not know nor did your fathers know, that He might make you know that man shall not live by bread alone; but man lives by every word that proceeds from the mouth of the LORD. We'll dig into both of these Scriptures in more depth in an upcoming chapter, but what I want to highlight here now, in both passages, is "every word." We are to live by every word that proceeds from the mouth of God, and we know God's every word is the Bible, all of it, and that the Bible is Jesus.

Here are some Scriptures that give us a peek at whom and what Jesus is:

Jesus is our Redeemer – Job 19:25 "For I know that my Redeemer lives, And He shall stand at the last on earth;"

Jesus is our Chief Cornerstone – Psalm 118:22 "The stone which the builders rejected Has become the chief cornerstone."

Jesus is Immanuel (God with us) – Isaiah 7:14 "Therefore the Lord Himself will give you a sign: Behold, the virgin shall conceive and bear a Son, and shall call His name Immanuel."

Jesus is our Counselor, Mighty God, Everlasting Father and Prince of Peace – Isaiah 9:6 "For unto us a Child is born, Unto us a Son is given; And the government will be upon His shoulder. And His name will be called Wonderful, Counselor, Mighty God, Everlasting Father, Prince of Peace."

Jesus is our Mighty One – Isaiah 60:16 "…You shall know that I, the LORD, am your Savior And your Redeemer, the Mighty One of Jacob."

Jesus is our Righteousness – Jeremiah 23:6 "In His days Judah will be saved, And Israel will dwell safely; Now this is His name by which He will be called: THE LORD OUR RIGHTEOUSNESS."

Jesus is The Beloved Son of God – Matthew 3:17, And suddenly a voice came from heaven saying, "This is My beloved Son, in whom I am well pleased."

Jesus is our Bridegroom – Matthew 9:15, And Jesus said to them, "Can the friends of the bridegroom mourn as long as the bridegroom is with them? But the days will come when the bridegroom will be taken away from them…"

Jesus is All Authority – Matthew 28:18, And Jesus came to them saying, "All authority has been given to Me in heaven and on earth.

Jesus is our Prophet – Mark 6:4, But Jesus said to them, "A prophet is not without honor except in his own country, among his own relatives, and in his own house."

Jesus is the Son of the Highest – Luke 1:32 "He will be great, and the Son of the Highest; and the Lord God will give Him the throne of His father David."

Jesus is our Savior – Luke 2:11 "For there is born to you this day in the city of David a Savior, who is Christ the Lord."

Jesus is the Son of Man – Luke 19:9-10, And Jesus said to him, "Today salvation has come to this house, because he also is a son of Abraham; for the Son of Man has come to seek and to save that which was lost."

Jesus is the Lamb of God – John 1:29, The next day John saw Jesus coming and said, "Behold! The Lamb of God who takes away the sin of the world!"

Jesus is the Messiah – John 1:41, He first found his own brother Simon, and said to him, "We have found the Messiah" (which is translated, the Christ).

Jesus is the Bread of Life – John 6:35, And Jesus said to them, I am the bread of life. He who comes to Me shall never hunger, and he who believes in Me shall never thirst."

Jesus is the Light of the World – John 8:12, Then Jesus spoke to them again saying, "I am the light of the world. He who follows Me shall not walk in darkness but have the light of life."

Jesus is the Truth – John 8:32, "And you shall know the truth, and the truth shall make you free."

Jesus is the One Who Makes us Free –John 8:36, "Therefore if the Son makes you free, you shall be free indeed."

Jesus is I Am – John 8:58, Jesus said to them, "Most assuredly, I say to you, before Abraham was, I AM."

Jesus is the Door – John 10:9, "I am the door. If anyone enters by Me, he will be saved, and will go in and out and find pasture."

Jesus is the Good Shepherd – John 10:11, "I am the good shepherd. The good shepherd gives His life for the sheep."

Jesus is the Resurrection and the Life – John 11:25, Jesus said to her, "I am the resurrection and the life. He who believes in Me, though he may die, he shall live."

Jesus is The Way – John 14:6, Jesus said to him, "I am the way, truth, and the life. No one comes to my Father except through Me."

Jesus is the True Vine – John 15:1, "I am the true vine, and my Father is the vinedresser."

Jesus is our Friend – John 15:14, "You are My friends if you do whatever I command you."

Jesus is the Holy Servant – Acts 4:29-30, "Now, Lord, look on their threats, and grant to Your servants that with all boldness they may speak your Word, by stretching out Your hand to heal, and that signs and wonders may be done through the name of Your Holy Servant Jesus."

Jesus is the Judge – Acts 10:42, "And He commanded us to preach to the people, and to testify that it is He who was ordained by God to be Judge of the living and the dead."

Jesus is the Rock – 1 Corinthians 10:4, "And all drank the same spiritual drink. For they drank of that spiritual Rock that followed them, and that Rock was Christ."

Jesus is the Risen Lord – 1 Corinthians 15:3-4, "For I delivered to you first of all that which I also received: that Christ died for our sins according to the Scriptures, and that He rose again the third day according to the Scriptures,"

Jesus is the Indescribable Gift – 2 Corinthians 9:15, "Thanks be to God for His indescribable gift!"

Jesus is Head of the Church – Ephesians 1:22-23, "And He put all things under His feet, and gave Him to be head over all things to the church, which is His body, the fullness of Him who fills all in all."

Jesus is Peace – Ephesians 2:14, "For He Himself is our peace, who has made both one, and has broken down the middle wall of separation, having abolished in His flesh the enmity, that is, the law of commandments contained in ordinances, so as to create Himself one new man from the two, thus making peace."

Jesus is Lord of All – Philippians 2:9-11, "Therefore God also has highly exalted Him and given Him the name, which is above every name, that at the name of Jesus every knee should bow, of those in heaven, and of those on the earth, and of those under the earth, and that every tongue should confess that Jesus Christ is Lord, to the glory of God the Father."

Jesus is Supreme Creator over All – Colossians 1:16-17, "For by Him all things were created that are in heaven and that are on the earth, visible and invisible, whether thrones or dominions or principalities or powers. All things were created through Him and for Him. And He is before all things, and in Him all things consist."

Jesus is our Deliverer – 1 Thessalonians 1:10, "and to wait for His Son from heaven, whom He raised from the dead, even Jesus who delivers us from the wrath to come."

Jesus is our Hope – 1 Timothy 1:1, "…by the commandment of God our Savior and the Lord Jesus Christ, our hope,"

Jesus is our Mediator – 1 Timothy 2:5, "For there is one God and one Mediator between God and men, the Man Christ Jesus,"

Jesus is the Great High Priest – Hebrews 4:14, "Seeing then that we have a great High Priest who has passed through the heavens, Jesus the Son of God, let us hold fast our confession."

Jesus is the Author and Finisher of Our Faith – Hebrews 12:2, "looking unto Jesus, the author and finisher of our faith, who for the joy that was set before Him endured the cross, despising the shame, and has sat down at the right hand of the throne of God."

Jesus is our Advocate – 1 John 2:1, "…And if anyone sins, we have an Advocate with the Father, Jesus Christ the righteous."

Jesus is the Propitiation for Our Sins – 1 John 4:10, "In this is love. Not that we loved God, but that He loved us and sent His Son to be the propitiation for our sins."

Jesus is the Almighty One – Revelation 1:8, "I am the Alpha and Omega, the Beginning and End", says the Lord, "who is and was and is to come, the Almighty One."

Jesus is the Overcomer – Revelation 3:21, "To him who overcomes I will grant to sit with Me on My throne, as I also overcame and sat down with My Father on His Throne."

Jesus is the Lion of the Tribe of Judah – Revelation 5:5, "…Do not weep. Behold, the Lion of the tribe of Judah, the Root of David, has prevailed to open the scroll and to loose its seven seals."

Jesus is the King Of Kings – Revelation 17:14, "These will make war with the Lamb, and the Lamb will overcome them, for He is Lord of lords and King of kings; and those who are with Him are called chosen, and faithful,"

Jesus is Faithful and True – Revelation 19:11, "I saw heaven opened, and behold, a white horse. And He who sat on him was called Faithful and True, and in righteousness He judges and makes war."

Jesus is The Alpha and Omega – Revelation 22:13, "I am the Alpha and the Omega, the Beginning and the End, the First and the Last."

Jesus is the Root and Offspring of David – Revelation 22:16, "…I am the Root and the Offspring of David, the Bright and Morning Star."

Jesus is all of the above and even more, hallelujah! I understand that is an awful lot to take in all at once. But it's important to know who Jesus fully is, so that we can make sure that we are following the true Jesus, following Jesus the oasis, because Scripture tells us in 2 Timothy 2:15-17 "Be diligent to present yourself approved to God, a worker who does not need to be ashamed, rightly dividing the word of truth. But shun profane and idle babbling, for they will increase to more ungodliness. And their message will spread like cancer…"

Having worked in the medical field at an oncologist's office for years, I understand some things about cancer forming and spreading. Cancer is the growth of abnormal cells in the body and develops when the body's normal control mechanism stops working. Therefore, old cells don't die off, but instead grow out of control, forming new abnormal cells. Cancer metastasis is the spread of cancer cells from their primary location in the body to another region of the body. The longer cancer goes undetected and untreated, the more regions of the body it can and will affect. He who has an ear, let him hear what the Spirit is saying.

What also is very interesting over and beyond understanding cancer and the spreading of it mentioned in 2 Timothy, chapter 2, is that a definition of babbling is "talking nonsense". So, in essence, not shunning or rejecting the nonsense, has allowed a cancerous spreading of so many different mirages of Jesus to partake of while people trek through the dry places of the world.

Another important truth we must understand before we dig deeper into the oasis and the mirage, is that the whole Word of God is prophetic from the beginning to the end, and all through it God reveals His entire plan for mankind. Throughout the Bible, His plan for us is ever unfolding from the Book of Genesis in the Old Testament through the Book of Revelation in the New Testament. And again, all of it is Jesus.

Yes, the Bible is a record of history with actual events that occurred in the natural. There are many written accounts of numerous Biblical events recorded through historians outside of the Bible verifying this. But those natural events also carry prophetic connotations. Paul teaches us in 1 Corinthians 15:46 "However, the spiritual is not first, but the natural, and afterward the spiritual." And Jesus taught in parables of natural things to bring spiritual understanding. The reason this is so important to understand is found in Proverbs 29:18 "Where there is no revelation, the people cast off restraint…" The KJV puts it this way, "Where there is no vision, the people perish…" And the ESV explains it like this, "Where there is no prophetic vision, the people cast off restraint…" Also, along the same lines, Hosea 4:6 says, "My people are destroyed for lack of knowledge…"

May we ever grow in the knowledge, revelation, wisdom, and understanding of our Lord and Savior, Jesus Christ. Amen!

CHAPTER TWO

THE OASIS: PROMISE, FORMATION, AND FUNCTION

"An oasis is a fertile place where there is life that is fed from water in the midst of deserts or dry places. It's a fertile island of life in the ocean of extremely hot temperatures of the desert and is formed by ever flowing rivers of water beneath the surface of the desert, creating a spring fed pool of water at its center. Every once in a while, it does rain in the desert which in turn feeds the streams and rivers that sustain the oasis. Without the water, an oasis cannot survive. An oasis is not only a fertile island of life, but also gives, supports, and sustains life to all that have been dwelling in or traveling through the desert or dry places."

The Holy Spirit showed me that we find the promise of the formation of the oasis in the Old Testament in Isaiah 11:1 "There shall come forth a Rod from the stem of Jesse, and a branch shall grow out of his roots." And in Isaiah 53:2 "For He shall grow up before Him as a tender plant, And as a root out of dry ground." Here Jesus, the root of Jesse and David, is promised to bring life in the midst of a dry time and place. And in Revelation 22:16, Jesus Himself confirms it. "I, Jesus, have sent My angel to testify to you these things in the churches. I am the Root and the offspring of David…"

Furthermore, we discover the promise of the oasis throughout the Old Testament. Isaiah 41:17-18 "The poor and needy seek water, but there is none, their tongues fail for thirst. I, the LORD, will hear them; I, the God of Israel, will not forsake them. I will open rivers in desolate heights, and fountains in the midst of valleys; I will make the wilderness a pool of water, and the dry land springs of water. Isaiah 43:19-20 says, "Behold, I will do a new thing, now it shall spring forth; shall you not know it? I will even make a road in the wilderness and rivers in the desert to give drink to My people, My Chosen."

In addition, we learn throughout the Old Testament that water signifies the Holy Spirit whom Jesus the oasis promised us He would send after Him. Isaiah 12:3 says, "Therefore with joy you will draw water from the wells of salvation." Isaiah 44:3-4 says, "for I will pour water on him who is thirsty, and floods on the dry ground; I will pour My Spirit on your descendants, and my blessing on your offspring; they will spring up among the grass like willows by the watercourses. And we have Isaiah 55:1 "Ho! Everyone who thirsts, come to the waters…" As well as Isaiah 58:11 "The LORD will guide you continually, and satisfy your soul in drought, and strengthen your bones; you shall be like a watered garden, and like a spring of water whose waters do not fail."

We also are taught in the Old Testament that Jesus was in the beginning, like we discussed previously. Here we find Jesus was the rock, and that He was giving water to God's people in the desert as Moses led them through it. Psalms 78:15-16 "He split the rocks in the wilderness and gave them drink in abundance like the depths. He also brought streams out of the rock and caused waters to run down like rivers." And in Psalms 105:41 "He opened the rock, and water gushed out; it ran in the dry places like a river." As well as Isaiah 48:21 "And they did not thirst when He led them through the deserts; He caused the waters to flow from the rock for them; He also split the rock, and water gushed out."

In the New Testament we realize that the stream of water from the rock was also a prophecy of Jesus' coming and giving the Holy Spirit. 1 Corinthians 10:3-4 "all ate the same spiritual food, and all drank the same spiritual drink. For they drank of the spiritual Rock that followed them, and that Rock was Christ…"

The New Testament additionally teaches us that Jesus promised to send the Holy Spirit characterized as water, in the Gospel of John. John 4:7-14 says, A woman of Samaria came to draw water. Jesus said to her, "Give me a drink." For His disciples had gone away to buy food. Then the woman of Samaria said to Him, "How is it that You, being a Jew, ask a drink from me, a Samaritan woman?" For Jews have no dealings with Samaritans. Jesus answered and said to her, "If you knew the gift of God, and who it is who says to you, 'Give me a drink,' you would have asked Him, and He would have given you living water." The woman said to Him, "Sir, you have nothing to draw with, and the well is deep. Where then do you get that living water? Are you greater than our father Jacob, who gave us the well, and drank from it himself, as well as his sons and livestock?" Jesus answered and said to her, "Whoever drinks of the water that I shall give him will never thirst. But the water I shall give him will become in him a fountain of water springing up into everlasting life."

In John chapter 7 verses 37-39, we see again that water is the Holy Spirit. It reads, On the last day, that great day of the feast, Jesus stood and cried out, saying, "If anyone thirsts, let him come to Me and drink. He who believes in Me, as the Scripture has said, out of his heart will flow rivers of living water." But this He spoke concerning the Spirit, whom those believing in Him would receive, because Jesus was not yet glorified.

Then again in the Book of Revelation we find water signifying the Holy Spirit. Revelation 21:6-7 reads, And He said to me, "It is done! I am the Alpha and the Omega, the Beginning and the End. I will give of the fountain of water of life freely to him who thirsts. He who overcomes shall inherit all things, and I will be his God and he shall be My son." Revelation 22:1 says, "And he showed me a pure river of water of life, clear as crystal, proceeding from the throne of God and of the Lamb." As well as Revelation 22:17 which states, And the Spirit and the bride say, "Come!" And let him who hears say "Come!" And let him who thirsts come. Whoever desires, let him take the water of life freely.

As we discussed in the definition of an oasis, the water fed oasis gives, supports and sustains life for all who have been traveling through the deserts or dry places. The life within the oasis consists of reeds and other foliage as well as trees such as date palms, figs, olives, and apricots. The shade of the date palms helps smaller trees like peach trees to thrive within the oasis. And within the oasis, the trees provide food to eat right alongside the waters that give drink.

There are two points above that we should take note of. First, the tall date palms give shade for relief of the scorching sun that drains us of our energy when traveling through deserts and dry places and depletes us of the water our natural bodies need to survive and that our spirit man needs to survive as well. Now let's look at what we find in Psalm 121:5-6 "The Lord is your keeper; The Lord is your shade at your right hand. The sun shall not strike you by day..." Isaiah 25:4 puts it like this, "For you have been a strength to the needy in his distress, a refuge from the storm, a shade from the heat..." Psalm 91:1 NIV says, "Whoever dwells in the shelter of the Most High will rest in the shadow of the Almighty." These Scriptures are yet other descriptions of the Lord Jesus, our oasis. He protects us from the ravages of dry, sun scorched deserts and the heat of dry places by covering us with His shade and being our shelter. Thank you, Father!

The second point we need to realize is this. The trees in the oasis offer food for all to eat. The life in the oasis is the bread of life that sustains life to all who come to it. That's Jesus! And again, we find that Jesus was in the beginning from Deuteronomy 8:3 (Moses said) "So He humbled you, allowed you to hunger, and fed you with manna which you did not know nor did your fathers know, that He might make you know that man shall not live by bread alone; but man lives by every word that proceeds from the mouth of the LORD." Psalm 105 also speaks of this in verse 40. "The people asked, and He brought quail, and he satisfied them with the bread of heaven."

Jesus Himself taught us that He was, indeed, the bread of heaven and of life in John 6:32-35. It reads, Then Jesus said to them, "Most assuredly I say to you, Moses did not give you the bread from heaven, but my Father gives you the true bread from heaven. For the bread of God is He who comes down from heaven and gives life to the world." Then they said to him, "Lord, give us this bread always," And Jesus said to them, "I am the bread of life. He who comes to Me shall never hunger, and he who believes in Me shall never thirst." To sum it up, all who come to Jesus the oasis, will be shaded and sheltered from the desert, the dry places and parched land, and will never hunger or thirst because Jesus the oasis provides shelter, food and drink.

Every once in a while, it does rain in the desert which in turn feeds the streams and rivers that sustain the oasis. The word we want to focus on now is "rain". Throughout the Scriptures, rain represents both natural and spiritual showers of blessings. We find these precepts in the following verses. Psalm 72:6 reads, "He shall come down like rain upon the grass before mowing, Like showers that water the earth."

Hosea 10:12 says, "Sow for yourselves righteousness, reap in mercy; break up your fallow ground, for it is time to seek the Lord till He comes and rains righteousness on you."

Deuteronomy 32:2 states it this way, "Let my teaching drop as the rain, My speech distill as the dew, As raindrops on the tender herb, and as showers on the grass."

Psalm 68:9 says "You, O God, sent a plentiful rain, whereby You confirmed Your inheritance, when it was weary."

Hosea 6:3 states, "Let us know, let us pursue the knowledge of the Lord. His going forth is established as the morning; He will come to us like the rain, like the latter and former rain to earth."

Psalm 84:6 reads "As they pass through the Valley of Baca, they make it a spring; the rain also covers it with pools."

Ezekiel 34:26 states it plainly, "I will make them and the places around My hill a blessing; and I will cause showers to come down in their season; they will be showers of blessing."

Hebrews 6:7 says "For the earth which drinks in the rain that often comes upon it, and bears herbs useful to those by whom it is cultivated, receives blessing from God;"

The Bible also teaches us that it is God who prepares and sends the rain and does so for His purposes. Isaiah 55:9-10 "For as the rain comes down, and the snow from heaven, and do not return there, but water the earth, and make it bring forth and bud, that it may give seed to the Sower and bread to the eater, so shall My word be that goes forth from My mouth; it shall not return to me void, but it shall accomplish what I please, and it will prosper in the thing for which I sent it."

Psalm 65:9-10 shows us this as well, "You visit the earth and water it, you greatly enrich it; the river of God is full of water; You provide their grain, for so You have prepared it. You water its ridges abundantly, You settle its furrows with showers, You bless its growth." And lastly, Acts 14:17, "and yet He did not leave Himself without witness, in that He did good and gave you rains from heaven and fruitful seasons, satisfying your hearts with food and gladness."

We learn that the rain God sends is sometimes contingent upon our obedience to Him in the following Scripture verses. Deuteronomy 11:13-14 "And it shall be that if you earnestly obey My commandments which I command you today, to love the Lord your God and serve Him with all your heart and with all your soul, then I will give you the rain for your land in its season, the early rain and the latter rain, that you may gather your grain, your new wine, and your oil." And Leviticus 26:3-4 "If you walk in My statutes and keep My commandments, and perform them, then I will give you rain in its season, the land shall yield its produce and the trees of the field shall yield their fruit."

We will get into Jesus the oasis a bit more later on, but first, we'll discuss the mirage in the next chapter. In the meantime, let us proclaim, Blessed be the name of God the father, God the Son, and God the Holy Spirit! We thank you Lord for bringing us truth and revelation through Your Word!

CHAPTER THREE

THE MIRAGE: FORMATION AND DECEPTION

"The definition and explanation of a mirage is an optical illusion or phenomenon in which the image of a distinct object, like an oasis, is made to appear nearby where there is light refracted through a layer of hot air on the desert floor. Or an object, like an oasis, that seems to be just ahead, but doesn't really exist. It's a reflection of light passing through hot air that can trick the mind into interpreting and therefore believing the sight is something real."

In looking at the formation and deception of a mirage, the Holy Spirit showed me there are two main components we need to understand in order to comprehend what He is teaching. First, a mirage takes place in the desert and dry places. Secondly, that a mirage is formed by light being refracted or bent or twisted through hot air, tricking or deceiving our mind into believing something is real, when in actuality, it is not. Let's take a quick glance at the elements that form the deception of a mirage before we dissect it into further detail.

The first element we find is light and we know from the Word that Jesus is the light. Isaiah 60:1 "Arise, shine; For your light has come! And the glory of the Lord is risen upon you." Daniel 2:22 teaches us that He (God) reveals deep and secret things; He knows what is in the darkness, and light dwells with Him. We also find this in John 8:12, Then Jesus spoke to them again, saying, "I am the light of the world. He who follows Me shall not walk in darkness but have the light of life." And Revelation 21:23 (Speaking of the New Jerusalem in heaven) "The city had no need of the sun or of the moon to shine in it. The glory of God illuminated it. The Lamb is the light."

The second element we find is hot air. As discussed in the first chapter, in conversational language, the phrase "hot air" is defined as lies, exaggerations, and nonsense. We know that lies come from the father of lies and that the father of lies is the devil. We find this in John 8:44 when Jesus is speaking to the Pharisees, "You are of your father, and the desires of your father you want to do. He was a murderer from the beginning, and does not stand in truth, because there is no truth in him. When he speaks a lie, he speaks from his own resources, for he is a liar and the father of it."

The third element is the bending and twisting of the light, tricking the mind into believing something is real when it isn't. And this third element is the deception. 2 Peter speaks of this twisting in chapter 3, verse 16... "which untaught and unstable people twist to their own destruction as they do also the rest of the Scriptures." We see the warning of this in Ephesians 6:11, Put on the whole armor of God, that you may be able to stand against the wiles of the devil." The definition of "wiles" is strategies or tricks intended to deceive or ensnare. 2 Timothy 2:26 gives reference to the snares, "...that they may come to their senses and escape the snare of the devil, having been taken captive by him to do his will."

Now let's take a deeper look at these components and elements. First, let's look into the devil being a liar and the father of all lies. He tried to bend and twist the light in the beginning way back in the book of Genesis, chapters 2 and 3. Here we find Eve in the Garden of Eden where God had placed her with her husband, Adam. God told them they could eat of every fruit of every tree in the garden with the exception of one. The word of God was to not eat of the fruit of just one tree, and that was the tree in the middle of the garden, being the tree of the knowledge of good and evil. He said they couldn't touch it let alone eat of its fruit because the day they did, they would surely die.

Enter in the devil, that serpent of old, who the Bible describes as more cunning than any beast God had made. Here he comes to twist and bend the Word of God. He says, "Pfft! You won't surely die. God only said that to you because He knows when you do eat it, you'll be just like Him because your eyes will be opened, and just like Him, you will know both good and evil." Here, we should take note that up until this point, Adam and Eve only knew good because they were in the midst of God's creation and all that He created in the first week, He looked upon and called good.

In hindsight, we know God was speaking of spiritual death, but at this point, Eve didn't know that. And after hearing the twisted and bent word of God, she looked at the tree differently. She saw the fruit did indeed look like good food to eat, and she now knew that it held the ability to make her wise. She didn't know before that she wasn't wise. She didn't know until the devil inferred it by his distorting of the word of God. So, Eve gave into the temptation and partook of the fruit. But she didn't stop there. She gave it to Adam as well. What fun is it to sin all by yourself? God had already said that it isn't good for man(kind) to be alone. We all crave company, and we crave company that is the same as we are, just like the old adage "birds of a feather flock together". Let's pause here for a moment because this passage reminds me of the new "woke" culture today. "Your eyes will be opened" and "you will be like God, knowing…" Sounds familiar, doesn't it?

Fast forward and we find God displeased with Adam and Eve and we find Eve, now "wise", blaming the serpent for tricking or deceiving her. So, God declared war. He told the devil that from this point forward, He was putting enmity between him and Eve and he would be cursed as the lowest of all created beasts and crawl around on his belly. And now for a key part, he would eat dust all the days of his life. Where do we find dust? That's right, in dry and parched places, deserts void of rain or moisture from any source of water. And in Micah 7:17, we find the enemies of God's people will do the same, as they are from their father of lies, not the heavenly Father. It states, "They shall lick the dust like a serpent…"

Now that we have seen how the devil operates, let's look and see him try to twist the Word of God again. After Jesus had been revealed as the Son of God and baptized in water by John the Baptist, and after the heavens opened up with the Spirit of God resting on Him, we find the voice of God coming from heaven. After God spoke and confirmed John's message that Jesus was God's Son and that God was pleased with Jesus, the Holy Spirit led Jesus into the wilderness for forty days. In this Scripture from Matthew 4:1, wilderness is defined as a desolate place and a desert in the original Greek. Also, wilderness is often used to depict the desert throughout the Bible, as in the case when the children of Israel wandered in the wilderness found in Joshua 5:6. It says, "for the children of Israel walked forty years in the wilderness…"

So here we find Jesus had just finished fasting for forty days and nights in the desolate desert, a dry and parched place, and was hungry. Then the devil shows up on the scene to try and trick Jesus by bending the word of God. Satan knew what was spoken by the prophets concerning Jesus and Jesus knew what the will of His Father was. Of course, it was a Spiritual thing, but the devil wanted to twist it into a fleshly carnal thing just like he did with Eve, using the lust of the flesh, the pride of life, and the lust of the eyes.

Satan comes up to Jesus knowing He was physically hungry and says, "If You truly are the Son of God, command these stones to become bread." Now remember, back in the wilderness in the Old Testament, we learned the manna from heaven was a prophetic type of the bread of life. I also find it interesting that Satan tempted Jesus with stones to turn into bread, because also out in the desert, out of the rock flowed water for the Israelites to drink and we know that the rock was Jesus. We also know Jesus is our chief cornerstone.

Was the devil also just trying to stick it to Jesus in reminding Him he was thirsty too? It wouldn't surprise me a bit as Satan is just that cunning and evil. Anyway, Jesus answers back saying it is written that man shall not live by bread alone, but by every word that proceeds from the mouth of God. Here Jesus overcame the fleshly or carnal temptation by turning it back to a Spiritual truth with Scripture. The devil lost that round, but he doesn't give up.

He next took Jesus to the Holy City of Jerusalem, set Him up on the pinnacle of the temple and said if You are the Son of God, throw Yourself down, and here he quotes the word of God, because it is written that He shall give His angels charge over you and in their hands, they will bear you up lest you dash your foot against a stone. (There's that stone again.) Psalm 91, where this Scripture was quoted from, was the promise of God's safety to all who dwell in Him. The devil is tempting Jesus with the pride of life, the pride of being the only begotten Son of God, and because He is, God's angels will take care of Him so there's nothing to worry about in throwing Himself down. But Jesus answers back with Scripture, the commandment of God that was given to the Israelites from Moses while they were in the desert. Jesus quotes it is written that you shall not tempt the Lord your God. Ta-da! The devil's attempt is dashed again, but he still is not giving up. He is a very persistent little bugger!

Satan then took Jesus up to an exceedingly high mountain and showed Him all the kingdoms of the world and their glory. And he said to Jesus, all these things I will give you if you will fall down and worship me. Here again, the devil is trying to twist the word of God into the fleshly realm. He's hoping to get Jesus to lust with His eyes and get what would rightly be His later on through Spiritual means from His obedience to His Father's Word. As Revelation 11:15 says, Then the seventh angel sounded: And there were loud voices in heaven, saying, "The kingdoms of this world have become the kingdoms of our Lord and of His Christ, and He shall reign forever and ever."

The devil is probably thinking that this temptation worked with Sarah after all. She did give Abraham her maidservant to give him the promised son and Ishmael was born. It worked once, why not again? But this was Jesus, the Son of God Almighty that the devil was dealing with now, and it isn't going to work. Then Jesus said to him, once again quoting Scripture, away with you Satan! It is written that you should worship the Lord God and Him only shall you worship.

The devil then left Jesus. I like to think of him leaving like a whipped dog with his tail between his legs. But he would rear his ugly head again as he is always looking for an opportunity to deceive and trick any one of God's children. And after the devil left, praise God, the angels showed up on the scene to minister to Jesus. Thank you, Father, for always taking care of Your own!

Next, let's take a closer look at dry places. They are depicted as cursed lands without the Spirit of the Lord. We find this in Jeremiah 17:5-6, Thus says the Lord: "Cursed is the man who trusts in man and makes flesh his strength, whose heart departs from the LORD. For he shall be like a shrub in the desert, and shall not see when good comes, but inhabit the parched places in the wilderness, in a salt land which is not inhabited. Then in verses 7-8, desert land is contrasted to a fertile oasis. It reads, "Blessed is the man who trusts the LORD, and whose hope is the LORD. For he shall be like a tree planted by the waters, which spreads out its roots by the river, and will not fear when heat comes; but its leaf will be green and will not be anxious in the year of the drought, nor will cease from yielding fruit."

The Scriptures also teach us that dry land is where the disobedient live. Psalm 68:6 "…But the rebellious dwell in a dry land." As well as where unclean spirits hang out as found in Matthew 12:43 "When an unclean spirit goes out of a man, he goes through dry places, seeking rest…" Through these Scriptures, it is plain to see that arid, dry places are places void of the Holy Spirit and where the devil takes up habitation and rest. He lies in wait for someone void of the Holy Spirit to inhabit as they are a dry desert land.

It is important to understand that sometimes the Lord will lead us to or allow us to go through the wilderness and dry places, to speak to us in order to get our attention either to Him, back to Him, or for more of Him. Hosea 2:14 says, "Therefore I will allure her, will bring her into the wilderness, and speak comfort to her." He does this for His own good purposes toward us. He did this with David, a man after God's own heart. David says in Psalm 63:1 "…My soul thirsts for You; My flesh longs for you in a dry and thirsty land where there is no water." And in Psalm 143:6 "I spread out my hands to you; my soul longs for you like a thirsty land."

Now that the Holy Spirit has laid out the foundations of both the oasis and a mirage, in the next chapter, we'll see the comparisons between Jesus mirages and Jesus the oasis in even more depth. Thank you, Father, for the Holy Spirit who leads us into all truth just as Jesus promised!

CHAPTER FOUR

JESUS MIRAGES COMPARED TO JESUS THE OASIS

As touched upon briefly in the Preface, out in the world today, there are a variety of different Jesuses being followed and this is because there is a following of partial Jesuses, or Jesus mirages. Allow me to expound. There is a following of the Jesus that loves everyone no matter what they do and therefore, they cannot be separated from Him. There's the Jesus that is everybody's friend and loves everyone so He will never offend anyone. There's also the Jesus of all you have to do is believe in Him, ask Him into your heart, truly believing He's in your heart, and you're saved, and you'll be happy in this life and then go to heaven and live there forever when you die, and that's it.

There's the Jesus of all you have to do is confess Jesus is Lord and then the reaping in of all good things can begin because Jesus made a covenant with us telling us to sow some seed and we'll reap blessings of happiness and wealth and the desires of our hearts while we are on earth and then we'll go to heaven when we die. There's the grace Jesus so you can live your life the way you want, knowing no matter what, Jesus' love for you and His never-ending grace, have you covered. There's the carnal Jesus who came to the world for the sinners after all, and he knows we are carnal and natural beings because that is how He created us, and He wants us to be free in our flesh. There's the same as everybody Jesus who wants us to reach other sinners and tell them about Jesus too, so we must blend in with them and be like them in order to reach them. Otherwise, we'll offend them and won't be able to tell them that Jesus loves them too.

These mirage "Jesuses" were created from the twisting and bending of the Scriptures, taken from "parts" of the Word, from the Holy Scriptures like John 3:16 "For God so loved the world that He gave His only begotten Son, that whoever believes in Him should not perish but have everlasting life." From Psalm 136 where it states many times that His mercy endures forever. Maybe from Jeremiah 29:11 "For I know the thoughts that I think toward you," says the Lord, "thoughts of peace and not of evil, to give you a future and a hope." Or perhaps Luke 6:38 "Give and it will be given to you: good measure, pressed down, shaken together, and running over…" And Romans 5:8 "But God demonstrates His own love toward us, in that while we were still sinners, Christ died for us". And perhaps John 15:13 "Greater love has no one than this, than to lay down one's life for his friends." Also, from Mark 2:17 "… I did not come to call the righteous, but sinners…" Or John 8:36 "Therefore if the Son makes you free, you are free indeed." And 2 Corinthians 3:17 "Now the Lord is the Spirit and where the Spirit of the Lord is, there is freedom." Maybe from Matthew 7:7-8 "Ask and it will be given to you; seek, and you will find; knock, and it will be opened to you." Maybe from 2 Corinthians 9:10 "Now may He who supplies seed to the Sower, and bread for food, supply and multiply the seed you have sown and increase the fruits of your righteousness."

However, Jesus the oasis said in John 12:24-25 "Most assuredly, I say to you, unless a grain of wheat falls into the ground and dies, it remains alone; but if it dies, it produces much grain. He who loves his life will lose it, and he who hates his life in this world will keep it for eternal life." And He said in Matthew 7:13-14 "Enter by the narrow gate; for wide is the gate and broad is the way that leads to destruction and there are many who go in by it. Because narrow is the gate and difficult is the way which leads to life, and there are few who find it"

In Luke 9:23 Jesus said to them all, "If anyone desires to come after Me, let him deny himself, and take up his cross daily, and follow Me." Jesus said to the adulterous woman in John 8:11 …" Go and sin no more." He said in Matthew 26:41 "Watch and pray, lest you enter into temptation. The spirit is indeed willing, but the flesh is weak." Jesus also said in Luke 17:1 "It is impossible that no offenses should come…" Jesus said in Matthew 10:22 "And you will be hated by all for My name's sake. But he who endures to the end will be saved."

Paul tells us in Romans 6:6 "knowing this, that our old man was crucified with Him that the body of sin might be done away with that we should no longer be slaves of sin." And again, in Romans 8:5-8 "For those who live according to the flesh set their minds on the things of the flesh, but those who live according to the Spirit, the things of the Spirit. For to be carnally minded is death, but to be spiritually minded is life and peace. Because the carnal mind is enmity against God; for it is not subject to the law of God, nor indeed can be. So then, those who are in the flesh cannot please God." Paul also showed us in Galatians 5:13 "For you brethren, have been called to liberty; only do not use liberty as an opportunity for the flesh, but through love serve one another." And in verses 16-17 "I say then: Walk in the Spirit, and you shall not fulfill the lust of the flesh. For the flesh lusts against the Spirit and the Spirit against the flesh; these two are contrary to one another…" Again, in chapter 6:7-8 "Do not be deceived, God is not mocked; for whatever a man sows, that he will also reap. For he who sows to his flesh will of the flesh reap corruption, but he who sows to the Spirit will of the Spirit reap everlasting life."

Paul also taught in Romans 1:28 "And even as they did not like to retain God in their knowledge, God gave them over to a debased mind, to do those things which are not fitting." The KJV says it like this. "And even as they did not like to retain God in their knowledge, God gave them over to a reprobate mind to do those things which are not convenient." The literal definition of reprobate in the Greek is failing to pass the test, unapproved, counterfeit.

The above mentioned "different Jesuses" are just a brief overview of some Jesus mirages so you can begin to understand what is happening out in the world today, and some of these truths will be discussed in further detail in forthcoming chapters. But before we go on, there is one other "Jesus mirage" we should look at, because its presence is very prevalent in the world today. It is the "name it and claim it Jesus" stemming from a prosperity gospel.

I heard the Spirit say that this is the false teaching of His Word that is breaking His heart and comes from the spirit of the age. It is the snare of lies, babbling, and nonsense that has many entangled and hurts them the most. And because it is hurting people, it is hurting Him. I heard the Spirit say, "Reveal It! Compare it to My truth, shine My light upon it and be a partaker of its withering for it is preying upon the weakest and causing them to stumble and fall as they are ensnared and led into dry places where there is no water of My Spirit. It is the teaching of the devil. It is a deadly mirage!"

Upon hearing Him speak, I thanked Him and sought Him and prayed for Him to reveal what He wanted me to write. I prayed that He would show me what Scriptures He wanted me to present to reveal His truth. He answered and showed me the following.

First and foremost, we must understand that the prosperity gospel is from Satan and not of God. We have learned that the enemy comes bending and twisting the Word of God. He does it because his goal is to kill, steal and destroy God's people. Jesus tells us this in John 10:10 "The thief does not come except to steal, kill, and to destroy." Then He tells us why He Himself came in contrast, "I have come that they may have life, and that they may have it more abundantly." Satan came to kill, but Jesus came to give us abundant life. Jesus knows how the devil operates. Remember how the devil came to Jesus and showed Him all of the kingdoms of the world and all of their glory and told Him all He had to do was worship him to get them? Right there we learned that Jesus doesn't promise us riches for serving and worshipping Him, the devil does that! The prosperity gospel is from Satan's playbook of twisted and bent light, not from the Holy Bible. Jesus, in Matthew 6:33, tells us to seek first the Kingdom of God and what? And His righteousness. And then what? Then all these things shall be added to you. See, if we seek Him and His righteousness first, then He will add abundant blessings to us.

Some leaders fell prey to the lies and began to teach in error. They taught that because God is a creative God and spoke into existence what He wanted, then so can we. There is power in God's words and because we are created in His image, we have the same power in our own tongues. Speak what you want, and you shall have it. Just name it and claim it. And, oh yeah, just sow your financial seed into my ministry and it will be multiplied back to you, pressed down, shaken together and overflowing. All you need is faith to believe it and receive it.

Yes, the Scripture tells us there is power in our tongues, but we need to be careful in what we speak. We should be speaking God's words. Proverbs 18:21 says, "Death and life are in the power of the tongue, and those who love it will eat its fruit. James 3:5-6 reads, "Even so the tongue is a little member and boasts great things. See how great a forest a little fire kindles! And the tongue is a fire, a world of iniquity. The tongue is so set among our members that it defiles the whole body and sets on fire the course of nature; and sets on fire by hell." And look at verse 8, "But no man can tame the tongue. It is an unruly evil, full of deadly poison." This is why we need to speak God's Word, as that is where the power is. I guess "name it and claim it" teachers never read those Scripture verses or ignored them as they just didn't suit. And perhaps they should read Proverbs 13:3 "He who guards his mouth preserves life, but he who opens wide his lips shall have destruction."

There is nothing new under the sun as King Solomon put it. Even in the Old Testament, God's prophets spoke out against greed and gain. Isaiah did against Israel's leaders in Isaiah 56:11 "Yes, they are greedy dogs which never have enough. And they are shepherds who cannot understand; they all look to their own way, everyone for his own gain…"

Let's take a look at Jeremiah, chapter 22. The prophet Jeremiah spoke out against the sons of Josiah. Josiah did what was right in the eyes of God, but not his sons. His sons coveted gain and abused the people whereas Josiah looked out for the poor and needy people. Verses 15-17 …" Did not your father eat and drink and do justice and righteousness? Then it was well with him. He judged the cause of the poor and needy; then it was well. Was not this knowing Me? says the LORD. Yet your eyes and your heart are for nothing but your covetousness…"

See, they have it all twisted and wrong. The Bible teaches that when we come to the Father through Jesus, He will use us for His purposes if we are willing, not the other way around with us using Him for ours. Now let's turn to the New Testament because the prosperity Jesus mirage sounds a lot like the destructive greediness that entered into the early church. Paul is teaching Timothy to beware of corrupt minded men who believed God was a means for gain in 1 Timothy 6:5 "useless wrangling of men of corrupt minds and destitute of the truth, who suppose that godliness is a means of gain. From such, withdraw yourself."

Then Paul continues again in 1 Timothy verses 6-12 "Now godliness with contentment is great gain. For we brought nothing into this world, and it is certain we can carry nothing out. And having food and clothing, with these we shall be content. But those who desire to be rich fall into temptation and a "snare", and into many foolish and harmful lusts which drown men in destruction and perdition. For the love of money is a root of all kinds of evil, for which some have strayed from the faith in their greediness and pierced themselves through with many sorrows. But you, O man of God, flee these things and pursue righteousness, godliness, faith, love, patience, gentleness. Fight the good fight of faith, lay hold on eternal life, to which you were also called and have confessed the good confession in the presence of many witnesses." And Peter warns us of the corruption of these mirage teachers in 2 Peter 2:14 "having eyes full of adultery and that cannot cease from sin, enticing unstable souls. They have a heart trained in covetous practices and are accursed children."

We must be very careful because this "prosperity believe it and receive it" Jesus mirage teaches that it's a matter of what we ourselves say and not what Jesus whom we trust says, but again, what truths we believe and assert in our own hearts. And also, that God's ability to bless us is only based on our own faith. But James 4:13-16 clearly contradicts that. It reads, Come now, you who say, "Today or tomorrow we will go to such and such a city, spend a year there, buy and sell, and make a profit"; whereas you do not know what will happen tomorrow. For what is your life? It is even a vapor that appears for a little time and then vanishes away. Instead, you ought to say, "If the Lord wills, we shall live and do this or that." But now you boast in your arrogance. All such boasting is evil. The Word also teaches us in Hebrews 13:5, Let your conduct be without covetousness; be content with such things you have. For He himself has said, "I will never leave you nor forsake you." We are to seek Jesus for who He is and not for what riches and material things He can give to us.

And speaking of Jesus, let's now look and see what Jesus our oasis has to say about it. In Matthew 6:19-21, 24 "Do not lay up for yourselves treasures on earth, where moth and rust destroy and where thieves break in and steal; but lay up for yourselves treasures in heaven, where neither moth nor rust destroys and where thieves do not break in and steal. For where your treasure is, there your heart will be also...No one can serve two masters; for either he will hate the one and love the other, or else he will be loyal to the one and despise the other. You cannot serve God and mammon." Jesus also said in Luke 12:15 "...Take heed and beware of covetousness, for one's life does not consist in the abundance of the things he possesses."

When talking to a young rich ruler who asked Jesus the good things he should do to gain eternal life in Matthew 19, Jesus, after telling him the commandments of God, in verse 21, added, "If you want to be perfect, go sell what you have and give to the poor, and you will have treasure in heaven; and come, follow Me." But when the young man heard that saying, he went away sorrowful, for he had great possessions. Jesus then told his disciples in verse 23, "Assuredly, I say to you that it is hard for a rich man to enter the kingdom of heaven."

Jesus also taught about a rich man and Lazarus in Luke 16:19-26 "There was a certain rich man who was clothed in purple and fine linen and fared sumptuously every day. But there was a certain beggar named Lazarus, full of sores, who was laid at his gate, desiring to be fed with the crumbs which fell from the rich man's table. Moreover, the dogs came and licked his sores. So it was that the beggar dies and was carried by the angels to Abraham's bosom. The rich man also died and was buried. And being in torments in Hades, he lifted his eyes and saw Abraham afar off, and Lazarus in his bosom. Then he cried and said, 'Father Abraham, have mercy on me, and send Lazarus that he may dip the tip of his finger in water and cool my tongue; for I am tormented in this flame.'

But Abraham said, 'Son, remember that in your lifetime you received your good things, and likewise Lazarus evil things; but now he is comforted, and you are tormented. And besides this, between us and you there is a great gulf fixed, so that those who want to pass from here to you cannot, nor can those from there pass to us.'"

And what really shows the heartbeat of Jesus concerning money and the mirage teachers of it, is found in Matthew 21:12-13, Then Jesus went into the temple of God and drove out all those who bought and sold in the temple and overturned the tables of the money changers and the seats of those who sold doves. And He said to them, "My house shall be called a house of prayer, but you have made it a den of thieves."

Is Jesus saying that no one who is rich or wealthy is going to have eternal life? Absolutely not! Just those that seek it before Him and love it above Him and those who take advantage of the poor with their false teachings about it, will not. There were some wealthy men and women who provided for and served Jesus with their wealth. They gave and did not love their wealth more than they loved Jesus. They sought first the Kingdom of God and honored Him with their possessions as instructed in Proverbs 3:9-10, "Honor the Lord with your possessions, and with the first fruits of all your increase; so, your barns will be filled with plenty, and your vats will overflow with new wine."

As Jesus said in Mark 8:34-36 "…Whoever desires to come after Me, let him deny himself, and take up his cross, and follow Me. For whoever desires to save his life will lose it, but whoever loses his life for My sake and the gospel's will save it. For what will it profit a man if he gains the whole world, and loses his soul?"

As a matter of fact, King Solomon, not only the wisest, but also the wealthiest of all kings that ever lived upon the earth, said that anything man chooses to seek over God and obedience to His Word, was all vanity. He had this to say in Ecclesiastes 12:6-8 "Remember your Creator before the silver cord is loosed, or the golden bowl is broken, or the pitcher shattered at the fountain, or the wheel broken at the well. Then the dust will return to the earth as it was, and the spirit will return to God who gave it. "Vanities of vanities," says the Preacher, "All is vanity." Then King Solomon sums it all up in verses 13-14. "Let us hear the conclusion of the whole matter: Fear God and keep His commandments, for this is man's all. For God will bring every work into judgment, including every secret thing, whether good or evil."

Also, if riches were a reasonable goal for us, then Jesus would have pursued it while He walked on the earth, but He didn't nor did He teach His disciples to either. His disciples went through many a hard time and did not take up riches for themselves. In that sense, they lived a hard life and most died violently in bloodshed. However, they counted themselves blessed to do so. It would do us well to remember that the cross was covered in bloodstains and not in gold, silver, and sparkly gems and jewels.

I heard the Holy Spirit say there is coming a season where He will cause a transference of a quantity of wealth of the world, to His church. He is our Father who owns everything and desires for His people, His sons and daughters, to be a people of blessing for His purposes, for reaching the lost and ministering to them and bringing them into His Kingdom. However, we need to be a perfect and mature body of Christ, fully prepared to serve Him with that wealth, not serve ourselves with it. In serving ourselves with financial blessings we will, perhaps unwittingly, destroy ourselves. This is why it is of utmost importance that we have the right mindset regarding finances, loving and serving the Lord more than loving and serving money and ourselves as again, Matthew 6:33 teaches us. "But seek first the kingdom of God and His righteousness, and all these things shall be added to you."

Sweet Jesus, thank you for leading us into all truth that we may abide in You, our oasis, as David wrote in Psalm 23:1-3 "The LORD is my shepherd; I shall not want. He makes me to lie down in green pastures; He leads me beside the still waters. He restores my soul; He leads me in paths of righteousness for His name's sake."

CHAPTER FIVE

NOT EVERYONE WHO SAYS TO ME LORD, LORD

During one of my times of prayer and seeking Jesus as He was giving me what He wanted me to write about, He gave me Matthew 7:21-23. It says, "Not everyone who says to Me, 'Lord, Lord,' shall enter the kingdom of heaven, but he who does the will of My Father in heaven. Many will say to Me in that day, 'Lord, Lord, have we not prophesied in Your name, cast out demons in Your name, and done many wonders in Your name?' And I will declare to them, 'I never knew you; depart from Me, you who practice lawlessness!'"

As I pondered upon this, I was aware of how easily many could be led astray by the prophesies, the casting out of demons and the wonders performed, that are mentioned in this Scripture. So, I asked Him how this could be. I told Him I knew that there was power in His name and that He says in John 14:14 "If you ask anything in My name, I will do it." And in Matthew 18:18-19 that says, "Again I say to you that if two of you agree on earth concerning anything they ask, it will be done for them by My Father in heaven. For where two or three are gathered together in My name, I am there in the midst of them." Jesus then answered me and said, "Yes, there is power in My name, but that isn't all of it."

So again, I pondered on this. I was having trouble comprehending that some prophesied, cast out demons, and worked wonders in the name of Jesus, but were not allowed to enter into the kingdom of heaven because they weren't one of His. I was contemplating on the part where they asked if they hadn't prophesied in His name. How could they prophesy in His name and not be one of His? I then heard Jesus say, "Even a donkey spoke to Balaam when God wanted him to. God can use anyone to speak His word to a person that He wants to hear it. Haven't you heard a word spoken through another and have My Holy Spirit quicken it to your spirit and you knew beyond a shadow of a doubt that you had heard from God?"

I answered, "Yes, on more than one occasion. The first one that comes to mind is when I heard God speaking to me through my then, mother-in-law to be."

God does say in Isaiah 55:11 "So shall My word be that goes forth from My mouth; it shall not return to me void, but shall accomplish what I please, and prosper in the thing for which I sent it."

I also remembered Romans 11:29 "For the gifts and calling of God are irrevocable." I thought about the gifts of God being irrevocable; that is, that He does not take them back. When God gives us a gift, He does so freely through His unconditional love and what He determined we would be before setting the foundation of the earth. When He creates us for a purpose, He gives us the gifts and talents we will need in order to accomplish that purpose in Him. He desires for us to use those giftings for good. And just like with Moses who said he was slow of speech and tongue, Mary Magdalene who Jesus healed of seven demons, and Paul who persecuted the Christians before his Jesus encounter on the Damascus Road, God used and still uses flawed, struggling people to accomplish His greatest work. The truth is, God can and will use absolutely anyone, believers and nonbelievers alike, to accomplish His purposes.

God's gifts are given for the benefit of building up His kingdom. Even if through our free will, we choose not to use the gifts God gives us for His good purpose, He still does not take those gifts back. Some may even use them not ever giving glory to God for them. Think of secular singers, for example. You hear them sing and they reveal a God truth, and you even recognize an anointing. Or perhaps a movie that causes you to think of a truth of God although it is not earmarked a "Christian movie." Or perhaps the same thing even in a book you read that wasn't written by a Christian. And sadly, there are prophets who prophesy for money, seeking glory for only themselves, selling the gift of God for profit.

But these things do not mean the person with the gifting is given eternal life. Every good gift comes from Father God in heaven. James 1:17 says "Every good gift and every perfect gift is from above, and comes down from the Father of lights, with whom there is no variation or shadow of turning." Matthew 5:45 says, "…for He makes His sun rise on the evil and on the good and sends rain on the just and on the unjust."

The above all made perfect sense to me, but I still could not get the Matthew 7 Scriptures out of my mind. They would pop back into my head for days and my mind would chew on them some more. Because of this, I knew there was more Jesus wanted me to understand about it, so I began pondering some more and as I considered, I heard Him say to me, "I want you to cover this whole Scripture, all the facets of it, so that it is made plain and there will be no room for stumbling because of it. For the time is coming when many will do just as is written in these Scriptures and will lead many astray. Even now, they do it."

Upon hearing this, I went back and read the Scripture again. This time the part that jumped out at me was when they asked, haven't we done many wonders in Your name. When I read the word wonders, the phrase "signs and wonders" came to mind. I knew signs and wonders were supernatural manifestations or miracles. When I thought of miracles, healings came to mind like the blind made to see, the lame to walk, the barren women to bring forth babies, and people healed from diseases that are known to lead to and cause death, diseases for which there is no cure.

I was wracking my brain on how this could be if these people who performed these wonders weren't one of Jesus' own. Then I heard Jesus speak again. He told me that I was forgetting the other half of the equation. I asked Him what He meant, and He explained when wondrous healings took place, there were two parties involved. He told me I was forgetting about the other party, the receiver, and that the receiver received because of their "faith" in the power of His name.

He reminded me of the woman with the issue of blood in Mark 25:21-34. It reads, Now a certain woman had a flow of blood for twelve years and had suffered many things from many physicians. She had spent all that she had and was no better, but rather worse. When she heard about Jesus, she came behind Him in the crowd and touched His garment. For she said, "If only I may touch His clothes, I shall be made well."

Immediately the fountain of her blood was dried up, and she felt in her body that she was healed of the affliction. And Jesus, immediately knowing in Himself that power had gone out of Him, turned around in the crowd and said, "Who touched My clothes?"

But His disciples said to Him, "You see the multitude thronging You and You say, 'Who touched Me?'"

And He looked around to see her who had done this thing. But the woman, fearing and trembling, knowing what had happened to her, came and fell down before Him and told Him the whole truth. And He said to her, "Daughter, your faith has made you well. Go in peace and be healed of your affliction."

Jesus also reminded me of the centurion officer's servant being healed in Matthew 8:5-13. It says, Now when Jesus had entered Capernaum, a centurion came to Him, pleading with Him, saying, "Lord, my servant is lying at home paralyzed, dreadfully tormented."

And Jesus said to him, "I will come and heal him."

The centurion answered and said, "Lord, I am not worthy that You should come under my roof. But only speak a word, and my servant will be healed. For I also am a man under authority, having soldiers under me. And I say to this one, 'Go,' and he goes; and to another, 'Come,' and he comes; and to my servant, 'Do this,' and he does it."

When Jesus heard it, He marveled and said to those who followed, "Assuredly, I say to you, I have not found such great faith not even in Israel! And I say to you that many will come from east and west, and sit down with Abraham, Isaac, and Jacob in the kingdom of heaven. But the sons of the kingdom will be cast out into outer darkness. There will be weeping and gnashing of teeth." Then Jesus said to the centurion, "Go your way; and as you believed, so let it be done for you." And his servant was healed that same hour.

Next, Jesus reminded me of the gentile Canaanite woman in Matthew 15:21-28. It says, Then Jesus went out from there and departed to the region of Tyre and Sidon. And behold, a woman of Canaan came out from that region and cried out to Him, saying, "Have mercy on me, O Lord, Son of David! My daughter is severely demon-possessed."

But He answered her not a word. And His disciples came and urged Him, saying, "Send her away, for she cries out after us."

But He answered and said, "I was not sent except to the lost sheep of the house of Israel."

Then she came and worshipped Him, saying, "Lord, help me!"

But He answered and said, "It is not good to take the children's bread and throw it to the dogs."

And she said, "Yes Lord, yet even the little dogs eat the crumbs which fall from their masters' table."

Then Jesus answered and said, "O woman, great is your faith! Let it be to you as you desire." And her daughter was healed from that very hour.

I then understood that the recipient's "faith" in the power of Jesus' name had everything to do with the wonders and was awestruck and delighted that He had showed me this because the faith of those receiving the blessings had never even once entered my mind. But even still, that Scripture kept coming back to my mind, popping in and out for several more days. So, I went back and re-read the passage that He had given me in Matthew chapter 7 and began pondering over the part when they asked have we not cast out demons in Your name. I was thinking that it couldn't be because Satan was casting out demons in Jesus' name because Jesus said in Matthew 12:25-26 "…Every kingdom divided against itself is brought to desolation, and every city or house divided against itself will not stand. If Satan casts out Satan, he is divided against himself. How then will his kingdom stand?"

As I was mentally chewing on this, the sons of Sceva popped into my mind, so I went back in my Bible and read Acts 19:11-20. It reads, Now God worked unusual miracles by the hands of Paul, so that even handkerchiefs or aprons were brought from his body to the sick, and the diseases left them, and the evil spirits went out of them. Then some of the itinerant Jewish exorcists took it upon themselves to call the name of the Lord Jesus over those who had evil spirits, saying "We exorcise you by the Jesus whom Paul preaches."

Also, there were seven sons of Sceva, a Jewish chief priest, who did so. And the evil spirit answered and said, "Jesus I know, and Paul I know; but who are you?"

Then the man in whom the evil spirit was leaped on them, overpowered them, and prevailed against them, so that they fled out of that house naked and wounded. This became known both to all Jews and Greeks dwelling in Ephesus; and fear came upon them all, and the name of the Lord Jesus was magnified. And many who had believed came confessing and telling their deeds. Also, many of those who had practiced magic brought their books together and burned them in the sight of all. And they counted up the value of them, and it totaled fifty thousand pieces of silver. So, the word of the Lord grew mightily and prevailed.

The first thing I recognized was that these Jewish men couldn't cast out the demon and the demon turned on them and tore them up. I remembered how Jesus said that demons can't cast out demons because they would divide the kingdom of Satan and yet, the demon turned on those brothers. Then I realized the demon must have turned on them because they weren't demon possessed. I asked Jesus if that was right. He answered me that it was, and I then understood it was by the power of Jesus' name, plus God's Word not coming back to Him void and the "faith" in the power of Jesus' name of those who were on the receiving end, was why those who weren't Jesus' own were able to cast the demons out in Matthew 7:21-23.

I heard Jesus tell me to go back and read about the sons of Sceva again and He would show me more truths. As I re-read the Scripture passages, I noticed the seven sons who tried to engage in the exorcism were the sons of a Jewish chief priest. I noticed they didn't say we exorcise you in the name of our father, Sceva, but in the name of Jesus, whom Paul preaches. I noted it had to be because they had not seen the power of God in their father, Sceva, but did in Paul. I heard the Spirit say that was correct and then He asked me why I thought there was no power from God in their father. I answered it was because he was a religious leader who didn't even really know about the power of God in Jesus, let alone know God or Jesus. He answered me confirming that was correct. I knew being religious and following rituals and traditions of men does not get you to heaven, nor do "religious leaders" who practice those things have eternal life either, so it made sense.

The next thing I focused on was the demon's response to the seven brothers when it answered back, Jesus I know, and Paul I know, but who are you? I understood the evil spirits recognized Jesus who has all authority and they recognized Paul who had Jesus living in his heart and being the Lord of his life, and had put on the Lord Jesus Christ, and lived to serve Him. I knew then Jesus was bringing out that we cannot get by with knowing someone else's Jesus, but we must know Jesus ourselves. Meaning grown children won't be saved because of their parents knowing Jesus, spouses won't have eternal life because of their husbands' or wives' knowing Jesus or any other relationship one may have with someone else who knows Jesus. Everyone must know Jesus personally, for themselves.

It was here that I recalled the last line of Matthew 7:21-23, "And I will declare to them, 'I never knew you; depart from Me, you who practice lawlessness!'" The word "know" in the original Greek speaks of an intimate relationship as with a husband and wife. It's an intimate relationship that goes both ways with one person of the relationship knowing the other personally and vice versa, in other words, one on one. It's the same with a parent and child, brothers and sisters, and even between close friends. It was the personal relationship Jesus was talking about when He declared to them that He never knew them in verse 23.

In Mark 3:35 Jesus said, "For whoever does the will of God is My brother and My sister and mother." Here, Jesus is teaching that a personal and intimate relationship with Jesus is determined by those that do the will of Father God. Ephesians 5:17 tells us, "Therefore do not be unwise, but understand what the will of the Lord is." In Hebrews 10:36, Paul says "…so that after you have done the will of God, you may receive the promise". Romans 12:2 says, "And do not be conformed to this world, but be transformed by the renewing of your mind, that you may prove what is that good and acceptable and perfect will of God". 1 Peter 2:15 says, "For this is the will of God, that by doing good you may put to silence the ignorance of foolish men." Jesus also said in Luke 6:46 "But why do you call me 'Lord, Lord' and not do the things which I say?" He said in Matthew 7:23 that they practiced lawlessness, meaning working contrary to law.

So now, we must understand what laws Jesus was referring to. And we find it in Matthew 22:36-40 "Teacher, what is the great commandment in the law?" Jesus said to him, "You shall love the Lord your God with all your heart, with all of your soul, and with all of your mind. This is the first and greatest commandment. And the second is like it: You shall love your neighbor as yourself. On these two commandments hang all the Law and the Prophets." Here we discover that it is all about God's love, a personal intimate love.

Paul, when speaking to the Corinthians in 1 Corinthians 13:1-3 said, "Though I speak with the tongues of men and angels, but have not love, I have become sounding brass or a clanging cymbal. And though I have the gift of prophecy, and understand all mysteries and all knowledge, and though I have all faith, so that I could remove mountains, but have not love, I am nothing. And though I bestow all my goods to feed the poor, and though I give my body to be burned, but have not love, it profits me nothing." This is because love requires an intimate, personal relationship.

We also find that James 4:8 says, "Draw near to God and He will draw near to you. Cleanse your hands, you sinners; and purify your hearts, you double-minded." Jesus also said in John, 7:16-18 "…My doctrine is not Mine, but His who sent Me. If anyone wills to do His will, he shall know concerning the doctrine whether it is from God or whether I speak on My own authority. He who speaks from himself seeks his own glory; but He who seeks the glory of the One who sent Him is true, and no unrighteousness is in Him."

So now, we, both you and I, have complete understanding of Matthew 7:21-23. Even though some called Jesus Lord, Lord, they were not going to be able to enter the kingdom of heaven, and yet, they were able to prophecy in Jesus' name, cast out demons in His name and do wonders in His name. Notice Jesus didn't deny those things were done in His name. We know they were done because the gifts of God are irrevocable and because of the power in Jesus' name, and through the "faith" in the power in Jesus' name of the recipients.

Jesus knows His own, but He did not know them. They didn't have a personal relationship with Jesus themselves. As a matter of fact, they practiced lawlessness in that they didn't love God with all of their hearts, souls, and minds. They couldn't love Him because they didn't even know Him. And those things they did in the name of Jesus they did, not out of love for God or Jesus, or even for the love of the people, but for the love of themselves. They were seeking their own glory and were filled with unrighteousness. Being filled with unrighteousness shows us they hadn't even repented of their sins because Jesus would have forgiven them their sins and cleansed them from all unrighteousness if they had. Here we also learn of just how deceiving a Jesus mirage can be.

Thank you Father for Jesus our oasis, thank you Jesus, for making this Scripture plain so that we can guard our own hearts with Your truth and also beware of "religious" leaders and teachers who present to us an incredibly deceptive mirage. Amen!

CHAPTER SIX

BEWARE OF THE FALSES

As revealed in a previous chapter, just the good parts of the Holy Scriptures cannot be selected and chosen to be the Jesus that we want. Is the foundational basis of all of those Jesus mirages, the actual Word of God? Yes, yes, they are. They are blessings and benefits from our Heavenly Father given to us when we dedicate our lives to Him, follow His commandments, and know and love Him personally. But unlike today's journalists in mainstream media, we cannot take bits and pieces of the truth and string them together, leaving out the truths we don't like, twisting and bending them to mean what we want. We cannot create our own narrative with the Word of God. In so doing, we create a false representation of Jesus. We create a mirage of Jesus.

When we compare Jesus the oasis with a Jesus mirage, we learn that taking out just the good parts of the Scriptures while editing out the parts we don't like and then fashioning all those good parts together, is the work of the enemy and not of the Holy Spirit. It is exactly what the serpent, the devil does. His punishment and curse for doing so, was to crawl on his belly the rest of his days and eat dust. And out there in the desert and dry places, creating Jesus mirages is his modus operandi, which in legal terms, is defined as a distinct pattern or method of operation especially that indicates or suggests the work of a single criminal in more than one crime.

The question that must now be asked is this: "How did so many different Jesus mirages come into existence and gain such a large following?" As the Holy Spirit touched on in chapter four regarding the "name it and claim it" Jesus mirage, they are being taught by "religious" leaders. We should not be at all surprised or shocked that there are so many "religious" leaders that are leading so many astray today. For Ecclesiastes 10:11-13 tells us, "A serpent may bite when it is not charmed; the babbler is no different." (Notice the formation of a mirage, the place where the serpent dwells, and the babbling hot air). "The words of a wise man's mouth are gracious, but the lips of a fool shall swallow him up; the words of his mouth begin with foolishness and the end of his talk is raving madness." And we learned of their message spreading like cancer.

False teachers and prophets certainly were around before Jesus in the Old Testament, and God was against them. Deuteronomy 18:20 reads, "But the prophet who presumes to speak a word in My name, which I have not commanded him to speak, or who speaks in the name of other gods, that prophet shall die." We can see that God is very serious about this and means business!

Let's now look at what God says in Ezekiel 13:2-9 "Son of man, prophesy against the prophets of Israel who prophesy, and say to those who prophesy out of their own heart, 'Hear the word of the LORD!'" Thus says the LORD GOD: "Woe to the foolish prophets, who follow their own spirit and have seen nothing! O Israel, your prophets are like foxes in the deserts. (There's where the mirage is formed) You have not gone up into the gaps to build a wall for the house of Israel to stand in battle on the day of the LORD. They have envisioned futility and false divination, saying, 'Thus says the LORD!' But the LORD has not sent them; yet they hope that the word may be confirmed. Have you not seen a futile vision, and have you not spoken false divination? You say, 'The LORD says,' but I have not spoken. Therefore, thus says the LORD GOD: Because you have spoken nonsense and envisioned lies, (there's the bending of the light through hot air that forms the mirage) therefore I am indeed against you," says the Lord God. "My hand will be against the prophets who envision futility and who divine lies; they shall not be in the assembly of My people, nor be written in the record of the house of Israel, nor shall they enter into the land of Israel. Then you shall know that I am the LORD GOD."

Ezekiel 21:29 says "…they see false visions for you, while they divine a lie to you to bring you on the necks of the wicked, the slain whose day has come, whose iniquity shall end." This sounds just like the false leaders today who teach Jesus mirages.

Now let's look at Jeremiah. Jeremiah spoke during times that were hard, during difficult times that God had brought about for His purposes. But there were the false prophets the people preferred to listen to because they liked what the false prophets were saying better than the Word of the Lord from God's appointed prophet, Jeremiah. Jeremiah 2:13 says, "For My people have committed two evils: They have forsaken me, the fountain of living waters (the oasis), and hewn themselves cisterns — broken cisterns that cannot hold water." Jeremiah 6:13-15 reads "Because from the least of them even to the greatest of them, everyone is given to covetousness; and from the prophet even to the priest, everyone deals falsely. They have also healed the hurt of My people slightly, Saying, 'Peace, peace!' When there is no peace. Were they ashamed when they had committed abomination? No! They were not at all ashamed; nor did they blush. Therefore, they shall fall among those who fall; at the time I punish them, they shall be cast down, says the Lord."

Jeremiah 14:14 says, And the LORD said to me, "The prophets prophesy lies in My name. I have not sent them, commanded them, nor spoken to them; they prophesy to you a false vision, divination, a worthless thing, and the deceit of their heart." And Jeremiah 23:16-17 reads, Thus says the LORD of Hosts: "Do not listen to the words of the prophets who prophesy to you. They make you worthless; they speak a vision of their own heart, not from the mouth of the LORD. They continually say to those who despise Me, 'The LORD has said, "You shall have peace"'; and to everyone who walks according to the dictates of his own heart, they say 'No evil shall come upon you.'" In other words, they spoke lies and we know all lies come from the devil as he is the father of all lies.

Next, let's take a look at Zechariah. Here, after speaking out against false leaders, God has promised His people, through His prophet Zechariah, a king who will come and save them and restore them. It says in chapter 10:1-2 "Ask the LORD for rain in the time of the latter rain. The LORD will make flashing clouds; He will give them showers of rain, grass in the fields for everyone. (Jesus, the oasis) For the idols speak delusion; the diviners envision lies and tell false dreams; they comfort in vain. (Jesus mirage) Therefore the people wend their way like sheep; they are in trouble because there is no shepherd."

We also find there are false leaders and teachers in the New Testament as well. They are defined as wolves, dogs, deceitful workers, and those having a form of godliness, but denying its power. We find these references and warnings against them in the following Scriptures.

In Acts 20:29-30 Paul says, "For I know this, that after my departure savage wolves will come in among you, not sparing the flock. Also, from among yourselves men will rise up, speaking perverse things, to draw away the disciples after themselves." Philippians 3:2 says, "Beware of dogs, beware of evil workers…" 2 Corinthians 11:13 says, "For such are false apostles, deceitful workers, transforming themselves into apostles of Christ." And 2 Timothy 3:5 says, having a form of godliness but denying its power. And from such, turn away."

Romans 16:17-18 Reads, "Now I urge you, brethren, note those who cause divisions and offenses, contrary to the doctrine which you learned, and avoid them. For those who are such do not serve our Lord Jesus Christ, but by their own belly and by smooth words and flattering speech deceive the hearts of the people." 1 John 4:1 says, "Beloved, do not believe every spirit, but test the spirits, whether they are of God; because many false prophets have gone out into the world." And 2 Timothy 4:2-4 says, "Preach the word! Be ready in season and out of season. Convince, rebuke, exhort, with all longsuffering and teaching. For the time will come when they will not endure sound doctrine, but according to their own desires, because they have itching ears, they will heap up for themselves teachers; and they will turn their ears away from the truth and be turned aside to fables." (or to Jesus mirages)

As I was praying and seeking the Lord for direction concerning this book, He said to me, "Study the woes of Jesus." I have and will share with you what He has revealed to me, as He has asked of me.

But first, let's look at who these sects of the religious leaders were, to gain a greater understanding. When Jesus started His ministry in Israel, Sadducees were a fragmented religious group that brandished public power in nearly every aspect. These men hated Jesus and consisted of the Jewish aristocrats, the upper-class nobles of their day, known as much for their wealth and corruption as for their religious devotion. The Pharisees, on the other hand, were the main religious leaders of the country. They had incredible control over the masses of people. They were the most revered in Jewish religious practices, customs, and culture at the time of Jesus.

The scribes were the official scholars of the spoken and written law and the instructors and interpreters of it. We see this in Mark 1:21-22. It says, "Then they went into Capernaum, and immediately on the Sabbath He (Jesus) entered the synagogue and taught. And they were astonished at His teaching, for He taught them as one having authority, and not as the scribes." The scribes preserved the Scriptures by meticulously and painstakingly copying them. In the Old Testament, Ezra was a Godly "skilled scribe in the Law of Moses". The New Testament scribes were men taught to write. At first, they were just transcribers of God's law as well as being the synagogue readers. But they later became interpreters of God's law and had the responsibility to teach the five books of Moses to the Jewish people. They were sort of like our constitutional lawyers who interpret the laws of our constitution in court today.

Let us not forget that these men, the religious leaders of their day, thoroughly enjoyed abusing their power, prestige, and influence over their followers. Nor forget that leaders today are still subjected to these same temptations and snares of the devil. And since these men were highly exalted in their day and were well respected by others, we can then safely assume that these negative attributes were not only found in the leaders, but in some of their followers in the synagogues as well. Therefore, we all would do well to pay attention to the critiques of Jesus.

As I was reading through the "woes" of Jesus, I heard Him ask me what other word He used the most along with, "Woe to you scribes and Pharisees!" It was then I noticed Jesus followed His woes with the word hypocrites. So, I then began to research that word. The definition I found in my dictionary is this. The definition of a hypocrite is a person who pretends to have certain beliefs, attitudes, or feelings when they really do not. Then it gave an example that made me laugh. It was, "like an outspoken vegetarian who gobbles up bacon in secret". Yes, that made me laugh, but I knew that wasn't what Jesus wanted me to find. So, I then began to research the word some more. I found that the word hypocrite is derived from the Greek word hupokrites which means: an actor under an assumed character, or a stage player. It is derived from a word meaning to answer a reply, the acting of a stage player from a prepared dialogue.

Having loved the arts and participated in drama in high school and beyond, I could relate. I remember having to get into "character" to play the role of someone. I would have to thoroughly study their attributes and gestures and personality type. I remember having to meticulously remember my lines of whom I was portraying or playing. I had to follow the script and listen for my cues. I loved putting on a show for other's entertainment. That's when it struck me. The scribes and Pharisees were play acting what they learned from the Scriptures coupled with what they were taught by their fathers before them. They were just playing, acting, putting on a show, and therefore, they weren't being real. All we do as followers of Jesus should be consistent with what we believe and who we are in Jesus. Play acting a character is meant for the "stage of entertainment", not for the life and character of a true Christian and especially not a Christian leader.

Now back to the "woes" of Jesus as He calls the scribes and Pharisees out for the roles they were play acting. As I was studying these woes, the one the Lord brought to my attention was in Matthew 23:27-28 "Woe to you, scribes and Pharisees, hypocrites! For you are like whitewashed tombs which indeed appear beautiful outwardly, but inside you are full of dead men's bones and all uncleanness. Even so you also outwardly appear righteous to men, but inside you are full of hypocrisy and lawlessness." Luke 11:44 puts it this way, "Woe to you, scribes and Pharisees, hypocrites! For you are like graves which are not seen, and the men who walk over them are not aware of them."

In order for us to realize what exactly Jesus was condemning them for, we need to know what Jewish law said about dead people and graves and we find it in Numbers chapter 19. Verse 11 says, "He who touches the dead body of anyone shall be unclean. Verse 13 says, "Whoever touches the body of anyone who has died, and does not purify himself, defiles the tabernacle of the LORD. That person shall be cut off from Israel. He shall be unclean, because the water of purification was not sprinkled on him; his uncleanness is still on him." And verse 16 reads, "Whoever in the open field touches one who is slain by a sword or who has died, or a bone of a man, or a grave, shall be unclean seven days."

Have you ever smelled a dead thing? Maybe you went out into the garage or down to the basement and smelled a nasty smell, searched for the source, and found a dead mouse. Or maybe while you were driving on a warm day with the windows down, were overcome with a horrible stench, then saw a deer struck by a car, bloated and decomposing on the side of the road. As for me, when I was younger, I used to go running our dogs through the fields to get them ready for hunting season with my dad. Sometimes the dogs would come back to us after rolling in something dead, an old rotting carcass of some kind or other that they had found. The smell was so putrid, I would gag and almost throw up. The dogs were covered in blackish-green, slimy nastiness. It was the most rancid, nauseating and disgusting odor I have ever encountered.

Also, have you ever visited a cemetery and noticed some very large or tall and pretty ornate grave markers with statues on them or maybe noticed some gorgeous artistic carvings engraved upon them? You knew that the person whom they marked must have come from wealth and prestige, right? They stood out among the other more small and plain tombstones, didn't they? But here's the thing, underneath both the small plain tombstones, and the large ornate grave markers, lay a dead person. Jesus was telling the scribes and Pharisees that exact same thing, that even though they presented themselves to the masses as the most ornately decorated, the most pious of men, underneath their beautiful garments with enlarged borders, underneath their whitewashed tombs, there still lay unclean dead men.

To further bring home that truth, Jesus even used a Pharisee in a parable to teach the people. Luke 18:9-14 reads, Also He spoke this parable to some who trusted in themselves that they were righteous, and despised others: "Two men went up to the temple to pray, one a Pharisee and the other a tax collector. The Pharisee stood and prayed thus with himself, 'God, I thank you that I am not like other men—extortioners, unjust, adulterers, or even as this tax collector. I fast twice a week; I give tithes of all that I possess.' And the tax collector, standing afar off, would not so much as raise his eyes to heaven, but beat his breast, saying, 'God, be merciful to me a sinner!' I tell you; this man went down to his house justified rather than the other; for everyone who exalts himself will be humbled, and he who humbles himself will be exalted."

Because the scribes and Pharisees studied the law and knew it well, and therefore were devoted to ceremonial cleanness and purity, this summation of them by Jesus had to be truly and horribly repulsive to them. Jesus was telling them that they were full of rotting, decomposing, rancid, putrid nastiness producing a foul stench, and didn't even know it. And because of this, they were defiling the temple in the process. And they also were causing others who came in contact with them to be unknowingly unclean as well. But all the while, they were priding themselves on being not only clean, but the cleanest of the clean, an example that everyone else should behold.

Matthew 23:25 says "Woe to you, scribes and Pharisees, hypocrites! For you cleanse the outside of the cup and dish, but inside they are full of extortion and self-indulgence." Luke 11:39 puts it this way, "Now you Pharisees make the outside of the cup and dish clean, but your inward part is full of greed and wickedness."

And in Matthew 15:7-11 Jesus said this, after the scribes and Pharisees criticized Jesus' disciples for not washing their hands before they broke bread and ate. Jesus replied to them, "Hypocrites! Well did Isaiah prophesy about you saying: "This people honors Me with their lips, But their heart is far from Me. And in vain they worship Me, teaching as doctrines the commandments of men". When he had called the multitude to Himself, He said to them, "Hear and understand: "Not what goes into the mouth defiles a man; but what comes out of the mouth, this defiles the man. And Jesus expounds further in Mark 7:18-23, So He said to them, "Are you thus without understanding also? Do you not perceive that whatever enters a man from outside cannot defile him, because it does not enter his heart but his stomach, and all is eliminated, thus purifying all foods?" And He said, "What comes out of a man, that defiles a man. For from within, out of the heart of men, proceed evil thoughts, adulteries, fornications, murders, thefts, covetousness, wickedness, deceit, lewdness, an evil eye, blasphemy, pride, foolishness. All these evil things come from within and defile a man."

What Jesus was teaching is that it's a heart thing. The LORD says in Jeremiah 17:9-10 "The heart is deceitful above all things, and desperately wicked; who can know it? I, the LORD, search the heart, I test the mind, even to give every man according to his ways..." And whether we like it or not, our hearts and our mouths are connected. Jesus says in Luke 6:45 "A good man out of the good treasure of his heart brings forth good; and an evil man out of the evil treasure of his heart brings forth evil. For out of the abundance of the heart his mouth speaks." The reason this was so vitally important to understand was because of the whole reason God sent Jesus to us and what was to come later, after His death and resurrection. We find it in Romans 10:8-10, "...The word is near you, in your mouth and in your heart" (that is the word of faith which we preach): that if you confess with your mouth the Lord Jesus and believe in your heart that God has raised Him from the dead, you will be saved. For with the heart one believes unto righteousness, and with the mouth confession is made onto salvation.

So, the scribes and Pharisees were unclean and full of disgusting, putrid, rotting dead things, putting on a show, play acting a role as the example of their cleanliness and purity that others should follow. However, Jesus on the other hand, in drastic contrast, laid His hands on the unclean to make them clean. Matthew 8:1-3 tells us, When Jesus had come down from the mountain, great multitudes followed Him. And behold, a leper came and worshipped Him, saying, "Lord, if You are willing, You can make me clean." Then Jesus put out His hand and touched him, saying, "I am willing; be cleansed". Immediately his leprosy was cleansed.

So, the answer to the question of how did so many different Jesus mirages come into existence and gain such a large following can also be found with the scribes and Pharisees. Matthew 23:15 reads, "Woe to you, scribes and Pharisees, hypocrites! For you travel land and sea to win one proselyte, and when he is won, you make him twice as much a son of hell as yourselves." And the same continues on today as Jesus said it would in Matthew 24:10-12 "And many will be offended, will betray one another, and will hate one another. Then many false prophets will rise up and deceive many. And because lawlessness will abound, the love of many will grow cold."

And as Paul said in 2 Timothy 2:15-17 "Be diligent to present yourself approved to God, a worker who does not need to be ashamed, rightly dividing the word of truth. But shun profane and idle babbling, for they will increase to more ungodliness. And their message will spread like cancer..." Unfortunately, the cancer metastasis started way back with the Pharisees and their converted proselytes and is still spreading to different parts of the body today.

Lord Jesus, help us to guard our hearts, our direct connection to You. Let us learn from what you have brought forth. Garbage, filth and nastiness on the inside, then garbage, filth and nastiness out from our hearts and mouths, but Your perfect love on the inside, then Your perfect love out from our hearts and mouths. Thank you, Jesus, Amen!

CHAPTER SEVEN

NO STRANGE FIRE, NO SCHISMS, BUT UNITY

I heard the Spirit tell me to turn to the Scriptures that He would give me, and He would show me something new. He first told me to turn to 1 Corinthians 12:4-27. It reads, There are diversities of gifts, but the same Spirit. There are differences of ministries, but the same Lord. And there are diversities of activities, but it is the same God who works all in all. But the manifestation of the Spirit is given to each one for the profit of all: for to one is given the word of wisdom through the Spirit, to another the word of knowledge through the same Spirit, to another faith by the same Spirit, to another the working of miracles, to another prophecy, to another, discerning of spirits, to another, different kinds of tongues, to another, the interpretation of tongues. But one and the same Spirit works all these things, distributing to each one individually as He wills.

For as the body is one and has many members, but all the members of that one body, being many, are one body, so also in Christ. For by one Spirit, we were all baptized into one body — whether Jews or Greeks, whether slaves or free — and have all been made to drink into one Spirit. For in fact the body is not one member but many. If the foot should say, "Because I am not a hand, I am not of the body," is it therefore not of the body? And if the ear should say "Because I am not an eye, I am not of the body," is it therefore not of the body? If the whole were an eye, where would be the hearing? If the whole were the hearing, where would be the smelling?

But now God has set the members, each one of them, in the body just as He pleased. And if they were all one member, where would the body be? But now indeed there are many members, yet one body. And the eye cannot say to the hand, "I have no need of you"; nor again the head to the feet, "I have no need of you." No, much rather, those members of the body which seem to be weaker are necessary. And those members of the body which we think to be less honorable, on these we bestow greater honor; and our unpresentable parts have greater modesty, but our presentable parts have no need. But God composed the body, having given greater honor to that part which lacks it, that there should be no schism in the body, but that the members should have the same care for one another. And if one member suffers, all should suffer with it; or if one member is honored, all the members rejoice with it.

Next, He gave me Ephesians 4:11-16. It says, "And He Himself gave some to be apostles, some prophets, some evangelists, and some pastors and teachers, for the equipping of the saints for the work of ministry, for the edifying of the body of Christ, till we all come to the unity of the faith and of the knowledge of the Son of God, to a perfect man, to the measure of the statute of the fullness of Christ; that we should no longer be children tossed to and fro and carried about with every wind of doctrine, by the trickery of men, in the cunning craftiness of deceitful plotting, but, speaking the truth in love, may grow up in all things into Him who is the head — Christ — from whom the whole body, joined and knit together by what every joint supplies, according to the effective working by which every part does its share, causes growth of the body for the edifying of itself in love."

Once I had turned to and read both of those passages, The Spirit asked me what I thought they meant. I answered Him with what I have always believed they meant and had been taught in times past. I said, "Lord, they both speak of the gifts and offices of the Spirit and that You have given many different gifts to the members of the church. Not one is greater than the other so one should not think higher of himself than what he ought to because the same Spirit has given all. As a matter of fact, those gifts which aren't highly visible to men, such as prayer and intercession and administrations, for example, are just as important as the more visible gifts of teachers and pastors, for instance. And that each and every one is important for the body so that all of the members of the church can be taught, trained, and equipped to do the work that You have called them to do. We are all one body, with Jesus being the head of us all. And in so doing, everybody can be on the same page, so that the whole body would be in unity in understanding with no arguments or disputes that could lead to all kinds of actions causing trouble not becoming of men and women of God."

Then He asked me, "And by the body, you are referring to a church or a group of churches belonging to a certain set of beliefs they have aligned themselves with?" I answered yes. Then He asked me a question that instantly brought revelation to those Scriptures that I had not understood before. He asked me, "Then wouldn't that mean that Jesus would have to have many heads?"

I instantly knew that what He was showing me is that every single person who was born again was the body of Christ, the one whole body of Christ, and Jesus was the head. One body and one head. It's not like I didn't know that before. I've always known this from Scriptures that the universal church is Jesus' body, like when Jesus says He's been building His church line upon line and precept upon precept and that He was coming back for a bride prepared without spot or wrinkle or any such blemish. I knew that meant every single believer. But in respect to the Corinthians and Ephesians passages He had asked me to read, I somehow hadn't put that all together before.

As I contemplated this, certain parts of those passages began to have new meaning, or an enlightened meaning to me. First and foremost, that all of the different denominations with their own set of beliefs and protocols and doctrine and mission statements are walls of partition, schisms, divisions, in the whole body of Christ. When new denominations formed around another of God's truths being revealed and restored after the church dark ages, many leaders of congregations rejected the new truth and therefore rejected part of the body of those who moved and taught in the restored truth. In essence they were saying to that part of the body, "I have no need of you," just as Paul spoke about in 1 Corinthians 12:21.

I heard the Lord say, "I am doing a new thing, My Spirit is beginning to move upon the face of the earth, and I am bringing life to dead places. I will cause a rising up of my people that will have them working in one accord. They may not understand what I am doing, but I am doing it," says the Lord. "As wide as the gulf may seem, as high as the walls of it may seem, I ask is there anything too difficult for Me? My ways and thoughts are higher than that of any man, as far as the heavens are from the earth, they are. And I will come back for My church, My bride, without stain or defilement, without so much as one flaw, blameless and with no guilt, all moving in one accord just as a flock of starlings fly in one accord, as in a well-choreographed dance. I am the choreographer," says the Lord. "I am beginning to do it. I am going to tear down the walls of partition and division, the walls will come down and you will all be one in Me. Prepare and look for it," says God. "I shall perform it!"

When I understood that God was going to cause the body of Christ, each and every one who is born again, every single Christian from every background to move as one in the earth, I was overjoyed. I couldn't even imagine how awesome that would appear to the world and how that would draw in so many lost souls into His great harvest. How beyond awesome that will be!

As I thought on these things, I remembered that Jesus prayed for this, that we would all be one, in John 17:20-23. "I do not pray for these alone, but also for those who will believe in Me through their word; that they all may be one, as You, Father, are in Me, and I in You; that they also may be one in Us, that the world may believe that You sent Me. And the glory which You gave Me I have given them, that they may be one just as We are one: I in them, and You in Me; that they may be made perfect in one, and that the world may know that You have sent Me and have loved them as You have loved Me". The Word says in Hebrews 7:25, "Therefore He (Jesus) is able to save to the uttermost those who come to God through Him, since He always lives to make intercession for them." I believe Jesus is still praying for us to become one. Also, Jesus spoke of bringing the unity of His church, of His body together, in John 10:16. He said, "And other sheep I have which are not of this fold; them also I must bring, and they will hear My voice; and there will be one flock and one shepherd."

I knew that Jesus is our High Priest as many Scriptures tell us such as Hebrews 4:14 which says, "Seeing then that we have a great high priest who has passed through the heavens, Jesus the Son of God, let us hold fast our confession." Then in 1 Peter 2:9, we are told we are a royal priesthood, we are priests called to proclaim the praises of Jesus. It says, "But you are a chosen generation, a royal priesthood, a holy nation, His own special people, that you may proclaim the praises of Him who called you out of the darkness into His marvelous light."

As I was contemplating on these Scriptures, I heard the Lord say, "They called out "Strange Fire", which again sent me on a journey of seeking the Holy Spirit on what He wanted to show me. I first went to Leviticus 10:1 where strange fire is mentioned. The KJV reads like this, "And Nadab and Abihu, the sons of Aaron, took either of them his censer and put fire therein, and put incense thereon, and offered strange fire before the LORD, which he commanded them not."

The NKJV says it like this, "Then Nadab and Abihu, the sons of Aaron, each took his censer and put fire in it, put incense on it, and offered profane fire before the LORD, which He had not commanded them." Continuing on in verses 2 and 3, it says, "So fire went out from the LORD and devoured them, and they died before the LORD. And Moses, said to Aaron, This is what the Lord spoke, saying: 'By those who come near Me I must be regarded as holy; And before all the people I must be glorified.'"

After reading those Scriptures, I wasn't sure what God wanted me to understand from them. So, I prayed and read them over and over again and prayed some more. Then the revelation came. In these Scriptures, it was the very first time that there would be priests under Aaron, the high priest and that his sons were set apart to serve God, that the priesthood was being expanded. This was the formal introduction to and consecration of the Aaronic priesthood. It was very important for what God had planned for the future with Jesus being the High Priest and we being a holy royal priesthood on to God. As Hebrews 2:17 shows us. "Therefore, in all things He had to be made like His brethren, that He might be a merciful and faithful High Priest in the things pertaining to God, to make propitiation for the sins of the people." And in 1 Peter 2:5 "…you also, as living stones, are being built up a spiritual house, a holy priesthood, to offer up spiritual sacrifices acceptable to God through Jesus Christ."

So, we find all the people were gathered before the Lord during the offerings. God had given Moses precise instructions on how it was all to be done, concerning the fire being taken from the altar, the fire that was never to be allowed to burn out, and the incense for the offerings which he passed on to the sons of Aaron. Moses had already told them how they were to offer the incense on the fire from the altar. But rather they brought forth fire from a different source, offering strange fire and incense on the altar. God was not going to allow Aaron's sons' disobedience, serving out of order, serving their own way, to set precedence for what He had planned for the future.

We know that the fire represents God's presence and incense represents prayers of the faithful. We find this in the following Scriptures. Psalm 141:2, "Let my prayer be set before you as incense, the lifting up of my hands as the evening sacrifice." And from Revelation 5:8, "Now when He had taken the scroll, the four living creatures and the twenty-four elders fell down before the Lamb, each having a harp, and golden bowls full of incense, which are the prayers of the saints." And Revelation 8:3, 'Then another angel, having a golden censer, came and stood at the altar. He was given much incense, that he should offer it with the prayers of the saints upon the golden altar which was before the throne. And the smoke of the incense, with the prayers of the saints, ascended before God from the angel's hand.'

Every single one of us are to be priests to God offering up the incense of prayer which in turn mingles with the prayers of Jesus our High Priest, then continues on to God the Father. There is no way to the Father except through the Son. Prayer moves the hand of God, it changes things, it brings about miracles and signs and wonders and shows a lost and fallen world that God lives on and loves and cares for everyone that they may be brought into the fold of the Great Shepherd, Jesus, and when time is full, to the eternal kingdom of God. This is so important. The way we, as children of God, kings and priests of Jesus, represent God and Jesus to the world matters! What we pray matters.

We need to pray the will of God, and we need to pray for what His Word says. Jesus condemned the Pharisees for their pompous prayers and instructed the people to do what the Pharisees taught, but not to do as they did. James 4:3 says, "You ask and do not receive, because you ask amiss, that you may spend it on your pleasures." We cannot do it any old way. We cannot present to the people of the world what way we may think within our own selves is the right way for our own pleasures. Proverbs 14:12 says, "There is a way that seems right to a man, but its end is the way of death." We have to do it God's way and be open to His Spirit moving and teaching us what God is doing in the here and now, in this present season.

Each and every one of us must be equipped for what God has called us to be and do, equipped by the apostles, prophets, evangelists, and pastors and teachers, for the work of ministry, for the edifying of the body of Christ, till we all come to the unity of the faith and of the knowledge of the Son of God, to a perfect man, to the measure of the statute of the fullness of Christ. And there is the key, unity. We all have to do it the way God instructs. We all have to do it God's way. And when we don't, we are out of order, and we offer "strange fire."

Once I completely understood all of that, I understood what the Lord meant when He said they called out strange fire. Once His truths began to be restored after the dark ages of the church, some of God's people grew comfortable with a truth, so much so that when God restored another truth, they didn't want it. They rejected it. They said they had no need of that member of the body of Christ, and they called the new move and truth "strange fire" as an excuse not to hear and seek to understand what the Spirit of the Lord was saying and doing because they were comfortable with what He had done already. And it happened with the next truth, and so on and so on, so that today, there are many different denominations and sets of beliefs and protocols and dogma and doctrine and mission statements, causing many schisms and Jesus mirages.

I find this so truly sad because as one reads through the whole Bible, God was always doing something new, adding something more, line upon line and precept upon precept and He will continue to do so until the end when we all come to the unity of His body and Jesus returns for His bride. I can't understand why anyone could not possibly want more of God. He is so good, His presence so amazing, His works so marvelous and wonderful, beyond compare to anything!

In some people's minds, anything strange can be associated with being demonic, unclean, possessed, or as drunkenness even when the source of the strange behavior is God. Matthew 11:18-19 says, "For John came neither eating nor drinking, and they say, 'He has a demon.' The Son of Man came eating and drinking and they say, 'Look, a glutton and a winebibber, a friend of tax collectors and sinners!' But wisdom is justified by her children." Matthew 12:24 says, Now when the Pharisees heard it, they said, "This fellow does not cast out demons except by Beelzebub, the ruler of the demons." And in Matthew 10:25 Jesus shares that if they accused Him of being strange and unclean, then they would do the same to all of us from His household. It reads, "It is enough for a disciple that he be like his teacher, and a servant like his master. If they called the master of the house Beelzebub, how much more will they call those of his household!"

Then we find they say Jesus is suffering from madness in John 10:20. And many of them said, "He has a demon and is mad. Why do you listen to Him?" Also, when the Holy Spirit fell on the disciples and they began to speak in other tongues, they were accused of being drunk in Acts 2:13 that reads, Others mocking said, "They are full of new wine."

I heard the Spirit say that the fire that went out from the Lord and consumed the sons of Aaron, the priests that stood before the people and Him, and offered the profane thing, doing their priestly duty through their own will and wisdom, is still a fire that will consume those like them. However, now that consuming fire is the lake of fire the Son of Man speaks of saying, depart from Me you cursed, into the everlasting fire prepared for the devil and his angels.

To show how very solemn and serious this is, the Lord showed me what He decreed against the profane priests in Malachi 2:1-3, 7, and 17. It says, "And now, O priests, this commandment is for you. If you will not hear, and if you will not take it to heart, to give glory to My name," says the Lord of Hosts, "I will send a curse upon you, and I will curse your blessings. Yes, I have cursed them already, because you do not take it to heart. Behold, I will rebuke your descendants and spread refuse on your faces, the refuse of your solemn feasts; and one will take you away with it. Then you shall know that I have sent this commandment to you, that My covenant with Levi may continue," says the Lord of Hosts... "For the lips of a priest should keep knowledge, and people should seek the law from his mouth; For he is the messenger of the LORD of Hosts...You have wearied the LORD with your words; yet you say, 'Everyone who does evil is good in the sight of the LORD, and He delights in them,' or, 'Where is the God of justice?'"

Wow! God was as serious as He could be regarding these wayward priests. They were supposed to represent God to the people and the people to God, and they failed to do so according to God's commandments. They were supposed to be God's representatives to carry out the spiritual things on this earth. God had given the priests the authority to bless the people, but now their blessing will be turned to a curse. They will be cursed themselves, because of their unfaithfulness to God. They had no longer looked at their priestly ministry as a holy call upon their lives, but as a means to make a living, a mere job like any other. And they therefore just went through the motions without putting their heart into it and without giving God the respect and glory He deserved.

In verse 3, God gets very graphic and uses harsh language to show them how He viewed them and let them know they were only worthy of the most unthinkable disgrace. The smearing of refuse, or dung, or excrement, or manure, or poop on their faces! Then they would be carried away with that poop. Back then, the waste or dung of the sacrificial animal was to be carried outside of the camp and burned. Then in verse 7, He says why. "For the lips of a priest should keep knowledge, and the people should seek the law from his mouth; for he is the messenger of the LORD of hosts." Back then, the priests were the ones who were the messenger of God. Not only were they to represent the people to God, but God to the people by keeping His commandments which we know were prophetic in nature of the coming and purpose of Jesus, the sacrifice without spot or blemish to take away the sins of the world of those that believe. The priests should have never spoken their own words while they were ministering, but the Words of the LORD should have been what they ministered. They were to be carried away outside the camp like those today are carried away from and are outside of the Kingdom of God at hand.

In verse 17 we find a summation of why God was so angry and disgusted with them. It reads, You have wearied the LORD with your words; yet you say, "In what have we wearied Him?" in that you say, "Everyone who does evil is good in the sight of the LORD, and He delights in them," or, "Where is the God of justice?"

See, disappointment and disillusionment followed the rebuilding of the temple because the presence of God had not come to it when they completed it. The priests then began to live in apathy toward God. They became calloused and lacking in spiritual discernment. They had rejected taking right and wrong seriously. So deeply gripped by complacent self-righteousness, they had the audacity to disrespectfully question the Lord, implying that He seemed to favor the wicked and was indifferent about the righteous. Yikes! This reminds me of the Pharisees disrespectfully questioning Jesus.

God had lost patience with this evil generation. They said one thing and did another. They were representing to the people, a mirage of Jesus to come, not of Jesus the oasis. You see, it is what we believe in our hearts that pleases or displeases God rather than heartless words spoken by rote. These people had gone so far astray into sin, that they didn't even believe God honored obedience to His Word and would be coming to judge it. This is just like some of the Jesus mirages being followed today as we discussed earlier, especially the carnal Jesus mirage.

We, as the children and priests of God, having been brought into Jesus' fold and made new in Him, must walk in the Spirit and not the flesh. We have got to do as instructed in Colossians 3:5-11. "Therefore, put to death your members which are on the earth: fornication, uncleanness, passion, evil desire, and covetousness, which is idolatry. Because of these things the wrath of God is coming upon the sons of disobedience, in which you yourselves once walked when you lived in them. But now you yourselves are to put off all of these: anger, wrath, malice, blasphemy, filthy language out of your mouth. Do not lie to one another, since you have put off the old man with his deeds and have put on the new man who is renewed in knowledge according to the image of Him who created him, where there is neither Greek nor Jew, circumcised nor uncircumcised, barbarian, Scythian, slave nor free, but Christ is all and in all."

As I was typing out this passage of Scripture, the Spirit of the Lord brought back to my remembrance Ephesians 4:14 "that we should no longer be children tossed to and fro and carried about with every wind of doctrine, by the trickery of men, in the cunning craftiness of deceitful plotting," and "therefore there is neither Greek nor Jew" from Colossians 3:11. I asked the Lord what He wanted to show me through these. I heard Him say that Jesus warned of the last days saying nation will rise against nation, or ethnos against ethnos, or in other words, ethnic groups rising against ethnic groups and that this is a cunning craftiness of deceitful plotting, by devious men for their own wicked and selfish ambitions who are under the influence of the spirit of the age. There is no ethnicity in the children of God. This too is a division, a schism in the body.

I heard the Spirit say, "Now, more than ever before, is the time for my people to guard their mind, will and emotions," says the Lord." In the midst of racial uprisings, people will turn away from walking by faith, by the truth of My Spirit, to walking by sight, seeing race first and placing greater emphasis and importance on it than on my Spirit, and could be swept away in that worldly deception. Do not be deceived. This is contrived by deceitful men to bring dissention. My Word declares, in that day, if it were possible, even the very elect would be deceived. Watch, awaken, and do not allow it to be possible, for there is neither Jew nor Greek in Jesus, as you were all baptized into Christ, and have put on the Lord Jesus Christ, meaning you have been transformed from being children of the race that bred you, into being children of the Most High God who chose you. Therefore, you all are one in Me. Beware, beware! Let he who has an ear for hearing, hear what the Spirit is saying," says the Lord, your God.

Help us, Lord! Help us to realize that placing more importance upon the same race as our own, before anything else, is the pride of life, one of the enemy's strategies against us. We thank you Father God and thank you Jesus, for all that you have done and are doing for us. Help us by your Spirit, Lord, to become one, in complete unity, moving in the earth as you have planned that the world may see that we are one in You and be drawn to You. How marvelous are your works! Help us Father to hear and understand what Your Spirit is saying and revealing. In Jesus' name I pray, amen.

CHAPTER EIGHT

YOU SHALL KNOW THEM BY THEIR FRUITS

Just before Jesus forewarned us that not everyone who says to Him, Lord, Lord shall enter the kingdom of God, He told us that we would know them by their fruits in Matthew 7:15-17. It says, "Beware of false prophets, who come to you in sheep's clothing, but inwardly are ravenous wolves. You shall know them by their fruits…Every good tree bears good fruit, but a bad tree bears bad fruit."

To further learn what the Spirit is teaching, we need to go back to the oasis. When discussing the elements of the oasis, we learned that Jesus is the oasis. We know that the life therein consists of trees and foliage that are rooted and grounded in the midst of the oasis, Jesus. We also learned that the trees are fed and sustained by the water, the Holy Spirit, and bear good fruit. Ephesians 3:17 says, "That Christ may dwell in your hearts through faith; that you being rooted and grounded in love," Colossians 2:7 says, "Rooted and grounded in Him and established in the faith, as you have been taught, abounding in it with thanksgiving." Proverbs 11:30 says "The fruit of the righteous is a tree of life." Proverbs 12:5 says, "…the root of the righteous cannot be moved." And verse 12 says, "…the root of the righteous yields fruit."

So then, we are trees planted, rooted and grounded in Jesus the oasis and cannot be moved. And we have roots that grow toward the water, the Holy Spirit, to keep us continually watered and fed and strong and bearing good fruits! Hallelujah! Remember Jeremiah 17:7-8 "Blessed is the man who trusts the LORD, and whose hope is the LORD. For he shall be like a tree planted by the waters, which spreads out its roots by the river, and will not fear when heat comes; but its leaf will be green and will not be anxious in the year of the drought, nor will cease from yielding fruit." And Ezekiel 47:12 says, "Along the bank of the river, on this side and that, will grow all kinds of trees used for food; their leaves will not wither, and their fruit will not fail. They will bear fruit every month, because their water flows from the sanctuary. Their fruit will be for food, and their leaves for medicine."

Thank you, Lord! Even when the dry hot winds blow and other trees begin to wither and dry up, we know by Jesus our oasis that we shall remain rooted and grounded in Him, strong and watered and green by the Holy Spirit. And our leaves will remain green, and branches bring forth good fruit. We will carry your medicine, the cure for everything that ails others, and we'll lead them to You, the Great Physician. We will become a shining beacon of light in the darkness and able to offer that life and healing to others who are weary and thirsty and hungry from traveling down the dry and dusty roads of the ways of the world that offer no rest, peace, or life!

Let us now go back to John 7:37-39. On the last day, that great day of the feast, Jesus stood and cried out, saying, "If anyone thirsts, let him come to Me and drink. He who believes in Me, as the Scripture has said, out of his heart will flow rivers of living water." But this He spoke concerning the Spirit, whom those believing in Him would receive; because Jesus was not yet glorified. Jesus was speaking prophetically of The Holy Spirit who is now with us, and lives within us. And 1 Corinthians 12:13 says, "For by one Spirit we were all baptized into one body…and have all been made to drink into one Spirit." The Holy Spirit dwelling and living inside of the believer's heart is as a fountain of living water flowing from the pool of water at the center, out of which plentiful streams flow.

See, once we are washed by the water of the Word and have taken drink of that one Spirit, we become an oasis ourselves with those fountains of water flowing from our hearts too. But we must take care because then, in the same way, if we don't present the whole truth of the Word, of Jesus, then we become a mirage to the lost of the world just like the religious leaders were in the days of Jesus. He said to them in Matthew 23:13, "Woe to you, scribes and Pharisees, hypocrites! For you shut up the kingdom of heaven against men; for you neither go in yourselves, nor do you allow those who are entering in to go in." Luke 11:52 says it like this, "Woe to you lawyers! For you have taken away the key of knowledge. You did not enter in yourselves, and those who were entering in, you hindered."

To understand this better, we have to ask ourselves what the purpose of the Scripture is. Isn't the whole word of God to first point us to God and then teach us that there is no way to Him, except through His Son, Jesus, whom the Holy Spirit testifies of? The Bible teaches us that Jesus is the only Savior and therefore is the only way to the kingdom of God and to heaven. And yet, these scribes and Pharisees were refusing to acknowledge Jesus as the Messiah. They were rejecting Him, preventing themselves from entering the kingdom of heaven. And in publicly speaking out against Him and trying to prove Him a heretic, they were preventing the common people, whom they taught, from learning the truth either, cutting off their ability to enter in as well. Jesus said in Luke 6:39 "…Can the blind lead the blind? Will they not both fall into the ditch?"

Acknowledging Jesus as the promised Savior would mean they would have to humble themselves and admit to and repent of their sins, But they couldn't even see that they were sinning because they were so great and perfect in their own estimation and loved this great system, they had created for themselves. They therefore took away from the people the key of knowledge. They were creating a mirage and teaching that mirage to others preventing them all from entering into Jesus the oasis also. But Jesus on the other hand, sought His Father's presence and was teaching the common people how to do the same. Jesus was using the key of knowledge to make a way for the people to be born again of Spirit and water, teaching them the love, character, and will of God, teaching them about the oasis.

Therefore, we must keep the waters stirred up like the pool of Bethesda in John chapter 5, verses 3 and 4. They say, "In these lay a great multitude of sick people, blind, lame, paralyzed, waiting for the moving of the water. For an angel went down at a certain time into the pool and stirred up the water; then whoever stepped in first, after the stirring of the water, was made well of whatever disease he had." When the Holy Spirit is stirred up within us, the moving waters stay pure and clean and powerful, not becoming stagnant. 2 Peter 1:13 says, "Yes, I think it is right, as long as I am in this tent, to stir you up by reminding you."

In moving on, it is of utmost importance that we understand what being born again entails. When Nicodemus came to Jesus in the night to find out more about Jesus and His ministry on earth, recognizing that what Jesus did, could not be done without God being with Him, Jesus told Nicodemus that unless one is born again, he can't see the kingdom of God. Then Nicodemus asks how a man can be born again seeing as how he can't enter his mother's womb a second time and be re-born. Jesus answered him in John 3:5-6, "Most assuredly I say to you, unless one is born of water and Spirit, he cannot enter the kingdom of God. That which is born of the flesh is flesh and that which is born of the Spirit is spirit."

In Luke 24:49, Jesus expresses the purpose for being born of the Spirit, of the baptism of the Holy Spirit. It says, "Behold, I send the Promise of My Father upon you; but tarry in the city of Jerusalem until you are endued with power from on high." Now, let's look at Acts 1:4-5, 8. They say, "And being assembled together with them, He commanded them not to depart from Jerusalem, but to wait for the Promise of the Father, "which," He said, "you have heard from Me; for John truly baptized with water, but you shall be baptized with the Holy Spirit not many days from now." … "but you shall receive power when the Holy Spirit has come upon you; and you shall be witnesses to Me in Jerusalem, and in all Judea and Samaria, and to the end of the earth." From these verses we learn the baptism of the Holy Spirit gives us power, it endues or clothes us with power from on high, in other words, God's power. In Mark 16:16-17 Jesus, as part of the great commission He gave to His disciples says this. "He who believes and is baptized will be saved; but he who does not believe will be condemned. And these signs will follow those who believe: In my name they will cast out demons; they will speak with new tongues".

In Acts 2:1-4, the baptism of the Holy Spirit that Jesus promised them, came. "When the Day of Pentecost had fully come, they were all with one accord in one place. And suddenly there came a sound from heaven, as of a rushing mighty wind, and it filled the whole house where they were sitting. Then there appeared to them divided tongues, as of fire, and one sat upon each of them. And they were all filled with the Holy Spirit and began to speak with other tongues, as the Spirit gave utterance."

I sensed the Holy Spirit wanted me to share the importance of the gift of the Holy Spirit and of speaking in tongues as well as what it accomplishes, as I had been praying for an acquaintance of mine following what she said. She said that if someone tells you they have received the baptism of the Holy Spirit with the evidence of speaking in tongues, walk away. I instantly felt a grieving within my spirit as it was clear she was missing out on a gift that God and Jesus want us to have and she was encouraging others to do the same. My heart ached for her to know the truth and not be led astray, keeping her from knowing and experiencing the power of the Holy Spirit in her life as the Word teaches us.

First, we'll look at the Scripture passages that teach us that the Holy Spirit is a gift. Luke 11:13 "If you then, being evil, know how to give good gifts to your children, how much more will your heavenly Father give the Holy Spirit to those who ask Him." Acts 2:38-39, Then Peter said to them, "Repent, and let every one of you be baptized in the name of Jesus Christ for the remission of sins; and you shall receive the gift of the Holy Spirit. For the promise is to you and to your children, and to all who are afar off, as many as the Lord our God will call." Acts 10:44-46 says, "While Peter was still speaking these words, the Holy Spirit fell upon all those who heard the word. And those of the circumcision who believed were astonished, as many as came with Peter, because the gift of the Holy Spirit had been poured out on the Gentiles also. For they heard them speak with tongues and magnify God…"

I will never forget the day God gave me the gift of being baptized in the Holy Spirit with the evidence of speaking in tongues. After I had been baptized in water signifying the washing away and remission of my sins and being born into the kingdom of God as a new creature in Him, my pastor at the time told me he heard the Spirit of God tell him that He wanted to give me the gift of the Holy Spirit. I didn't even know what the gift of the Holy Spirit was, and I told my pastor just that, but followed by saying that if God wanted to give me a gift, I surely wanted to accept it, and I meant that from the bottom of my heart. He then laid hands on me and prayed that I would receive the baptism of the Holy Spirit. Then he told me to open my mouth and begin to speak in the Spirit. I did as I was told, and out of my mouth flowed what I can best describe as uttering strange syllables. Sounds that were strange to my ears and that I, on my own, could never replicate.

After that, Pastor told me to pray in the Holy Spirit as often as I could to strengthen the gift within me. I did as he instructed, and it was after that the Holy Spirit began to speak to me, telling me things that were going to happen in my and my husband's lives and then they came to pass. Scripture in my Bible began to have new meaning to me as well, as the Holy Spirit brought revelation to them in ways I hadn't understood before. Shortly thereafter, God gave me prophetic messages for our church congregation and many other gifts began to work in me as well. My life was changed and has never been the same. Thank you, Father! And through the gift of the Holy Spirit moving in and through me, other's lives were changed as well.

I'll share a few examples of the power of God working in my life after receiving the baptism of the Holy Spirit as examples. When my son was just over a year old, I would take advantage of his nap time to pray and study my Bible. One day while I was reading the Word after praying in the Holy Spirit, I felt the Spirit invoke urgency within me, a sense of a looming danger, and at the same time, just somehow knew I had to go to my son. I flew down the hallway and threw open his bedroom door only to find him hanging by his neck from the cord of his window drapes next to his crib. The cord used to open curtains back then was a loop which has since been banned. I ran over to him and immediately picked him up. When I did, he began to cry, and I found an angry red mark around his little neck. He had woken up from his nap and for the first time, climbed out of his crib. In doing so, the curtain cord hung him by the neck on his way down. If not for the warning from the Holy Spirit, there is a distinct possibility that my son would not be alive today.

Another like incident happened with my youngest daughter when she was about four or five years old. Her daddy had bought her a little plastic toboggan when she had gone with him running errands. She asked me if she could go outside and play with it. I told her she could, telling her to take it in the back, as our backyard had a sloping hill. While my oldest daughter played in her room and my son was napping in his crib, I again took advantage of the free time and began my Bible study and prayer time. And once again, as I was praying in the Spirit, I sensed danger and just somehow knew it was my youngest daughter. I looked in the backyard through the glass door-wall and didn't see her. I then franticly ran and looked out the front bay window. There she was, at the top of the driveway at the edge of the road with a man in a pickup truck, passenger door open, in front of her. I sprinted to the front door, swung it open, and screamed her name, telling her to come inside.

At that point, the truck sped away, passenger door still open. My daughter grabbed her little toboggan and started back toward the house. When she was safe inside, she explained to me that she wanted to slide down the driveway because it was all icy and more slippery than the hill in the backyard and she could go faster. While she was sledding, a truck stopped at the end of the driveway and a man called her over to him as he rolled down the window. He told her he really liked her sled and thought his granddaughter would like one too. He asked her where she got it so he could go buy one. When she told him where her daddy had bought it, the man said he didn't know how to get there and asked her if she would hop in and show him as he opened the passenger door for her. She told me that was when I called her, and the man drove away. I won't even allow my mind to go to what may have happened if the Holy Spirit hadn't urged me to go to my daughter. I just praised and thanked Him for warning me through the Holy Spirit.

This next example involves the laying on of hands and praying in the Holy Spirit resulting in a miracle. My son was about six months old when he began crying non-stop. I could tell it was a result of pain. I was checking him over and discovered that his little tummy was tender to the touch as he cried out every time I pressed on it. I called his doctor who told me to take him to the emergency room. I then called my mother-in-law and she rushed over, picked us up, and drove us to the hospital.

After examining my son, they ordered an x-ray. They found a round glowing spot on the film and said it appeared that it may be a coin in the imaging. They thought that perhaps it was in his diaper, but after checking inside his diaper, found there wasn't anything. They then thought that maybe there was something metallic within the diaper itself. They removed the diaper from my son and x-rayed it, but nothing showed up. At this point, they thought my son may have swallowed a coin, so gave us a suppository to be inserted in his rectum that would clean him out. They explained this could take a while and therefore sent us home to administer it with the instructions of thoroughly examining the contents of his diaper once he emptied his bowels.

Once that was finished, my mother-in-law and I searched the contents of his diaper and found nothing. We were instructed to bring him back to the emergency room so they could take another x-ray. This new imaging showed the same metallic spot as before, and we were informed surgery would be required. At this point, I called my husband again and waited for him to get to the hospital. While waiting, I realized I hadn't even prayed for my baby yet, and then laid my hand on his stomach and began to pray in the Spirit. I prayed until a sense of peace washed over me.

When my husband arrived, we were told they had called in the best pediatric surgeon in the state so our son would be in good hands and that the surgeon was going over my son's chart and imaging results as we spoke. My husband and I waited and prayed and waited and prayed some more. Then the surgeon came in and told us right before prepping our son for surgery, he got an urge to do his own imaging before operating. He did and there was nothing in them. He showed us the x-rays taken before, compared to the x-rays he had just taken, and in the exact same spot where the image of a coin or stone was visible in the first images, there was nothing but a clear indentation of where something had been, but was no more. No one could explain it, but my son was released to go home. I thanked the Lord for the miracle of removing whatever it was from my son and for the Holy Spirit leading the surgeon to take his own tests before operating to discover it!

Another time while serving on the ministerial staff and prophetic team at church, after service, my pastor did an open altar call for prayer and a young man I had not seen before came before me for prayer. I laid my hand on his shoulder and began to pray in the Spirit for him and then pray with understanding. I prayed that God would let him know how much He cared for him and that He knew of his troubles. That God says He knows that he has been searching for a job and to not lose heart and trust in Him, because God had the perfect job for him. He just needed to keep searching, have faith and not give up, for God would take care of it. Right then, this young man interrupted me and asked me why I said that. I answered that I prayed what God led me to pray. He then asked, but how did you know I needed a job? I again explained to him I only prayed what the Holy Spirit led me to pray, and that I personally didn't know he needed a job.

He then explained to me that he had been looking for a job and was on the verge of losing his place because he couldn't make rent. And as it turned out, this man had been raised in the church as a small child but had walked away. He recently lost his job and had been seeking one, going on many interviews, but not getting hired. He was out of food and money and decided to come to the nearest church that morning. And praise God! Because of the Holy Spirit's leading in what to pray, that young man rededicated his life to God that morning and continued to come to church every Sunday thereafter. He was blessed with side jobs until he was hired full time and he not only didn't lose his home but found God and a new church home too! Hallelujah!

Next, let's turn to the Scriptures pertaining to the baptism of the Holy Spirit and speaking in tongues. First, let me make it absolutely clear that the baptism of the Holy Spirit does not make one believer better than another. There are no second-rate believers, no second-rate members of the body of Christ, in the kingdom of God. But rather, the baptism of the Holy Spirit gives an advantage to those who have received it. In the following Scripture passages, we'll see that the baptism of the Holy Spirit and speaking and praying in tongues gives us access to greater spheres or realms of God and that we deeply benefit from it.

1 Corinthians 14:2 says, "For he who speaks in a tongue does not speak to men, but to God, for no one understands him; however, in the Spirit he speaks mysteries." Here we learn that when we speak or pray in tongues, we don't speak to men, but to God. Not only do we speak to God, we are given access to the mysteries of God and therefore speak the mysteries of God. So, we enter greater realms of and receive deeper revelation of God. 1 Corinthians 14:4 says, "He who speaks in a tongue edifies himself…" and Jude 20 says, "But you beloved, building yourselves up on your most holy faith, praying in the Holy Spirit." Here we learn that we edify and build ourselves up when we speak and pray in tongues. We bulk up our spiritual faith and muscles, so to speak.

Also, Romans 8:26-27 says, "Likewise, the Spirit also helps in our weaknesses. For we do not know what we should pray for as we ought, but the Spirit Himself makes intercession for us with groanings which cannot be uttered. Now He who searches the hearts knows what the mind of the Spirit is, because He makes intercession for the saints according to the will of God." Here we learn that speaking and praying in tongues is communicating with God, spirit to Spirit and is the supernatural language given by God to believers. In other words, our spirits, the deepest part of us, speak with God's Spirit directly and therefore our praying in the Spirit is the perfect prayer because it accesses the heart of God and prays for His will, for what He wants done in the earth. It prays God's will be done just as Jesus taught us to pray in Matthew 6:10, "Your kingdom come. Your will be done on earth as it is in heaven."

Speaking in tongues is part of our spiritual armor of God and the way we can always pray without ceasing as we are encouraged to do in both Ephesians 6:18, "praying always with all power and supplication in the Spirit, being watchful to this end with all perseverance and supplication for all the saints", and 1 Thessalonians 5:17, "pray without ceasing." It is my prayer that these revelations from the Scriptures concerning the baptism of the Holy Spirit and speaking and praying in tongues strengthens your journey of a powerful Spirit filled life or perhaps, starts your journey toward it. Thank you, Father, for your Holy Spirit, who leads and guides us into all truth!

Now let's look at John 15:1-8 where Jesus puts a different spin on heavenly fruit bearing plant life. "I am the true vine, and My Father is the vinedresser. Every branch in Me that does not bear fruit He takes away, and every branch that bears fruit He prunes, that it may bear more fruit. You are already clean because of the word which I have spoken to you. Abide in Me, and I in you. As the branch cannot bear fruit of itself, unless it abides in the vine, neither can you, unless you abide in Me. I am the vine; you are the branches. He who abides in Me, and I in him, bears much fruit; for without Me you can do nothing. If anyone does not abide in Me, he is cast out as a branch and is withered; and they gather them and throw them into the fire, and they are burned. If you abide in Me, and My words abide in you, you will ask what you desire, and it shall be done for you. By this My Father is glorified, that you bear much fruit; so, you will be My disciples."

In these Scriptures we find that God is the vinedresser, Jesus is the vine, and we are the branches. I prayed after the Lord gave me this Scripture asking Him where the Holy Spirit fit in here, and He responded that the Holy Spirit would be the sap. Sap provides food, nutrients, and strength to the plant. We learned earlier that Jesus was also the root springing up out of dry land, and we learn that the root supports us in Romans 11:18. It says, "Do not boast against the branches. But if you do boast, remember that you do not support the root, but the root supports you." The root of a plant circulates the sap which is essential for the flourishing and fruitfulness of the branches. So, through Jesus, the root and vine, comes all support systems and supplies including the Holy Spirit, the sap, which we, the branches, require to bear good fruit. And we will continue bearing good fruit as long as we abide in Jesus and Jesus abides in us. Abide means remain, dwell, live, continue, tarry or endure.

To sum up what the Spirit is teaching here, we know that Father God is the vinedresser or the gardener of the whole earth. He has His eye on all of the branches of the vine and He keeps His eye on the fruit of them. He prunes the branches and watches over them making sure nothing hurts them while attached to the vine. Luke 10:19 "…and nothing by any means shall hurt you." By God's pruning process, we therefore become more fruitful, and He brings the increase. However, if we bear no fruit, it signifies we are no longer abiding in Jesus the vine, and those branches will be cut off and gathered to burn.

Pruning is a painful process, yes; however, statue masterpieces are never created with toothpicks and q-tips, but with hammers and chisels. Yet at the same time, the artist carefully and gently places his chisel knowing that too much pressure can cause damage to his masterpiece. It's like Paul teaches us in Hebrews 12:11. "Now no chastening seems to be joyful for the present, but painful; nevertheless, afterward it yields the peaceable fruit of righteousness to those who have been trained by it." And James 3:17-18 says, "But the wisdom that is from above is first pure, then peaceable, gentle, willing to yield, full of mercy and good fruits, without partiality and without hypocrisy. Now the fruit of righteousness is sown in peace by those who make peace." And Jesus taught us in Matthew 5:9 "Blessed are the peacemakers, for they shall see God."

In the next chapter, we'll move on to the fruit of the Spirit that Galatians 5:22-23 tells us about and study each of them in depth so that we will understand completely about the good fruit growing on the good trees that Jesus was teaching about.

CHAPTER NINE

THE FRUIT OF THE SPIRIT

Galatians 5:22-23 tells us what the fruit of the Spirit is. "But the fruit of the Spirit is love, joy, peace, longsuffering, kindness, goodness, faithfulness, gentleness, self-control. Against such there is no law. And those who are Christ's have crucified the flesh with its passions and desires. If we live in the Spirit, let us also walk in the Spirit."

The first fruit of the Holy Spirit mentioned is love. It is the greatest of all of the fruit of the Holy Spirit. We can't turn to our regular dictionaries to gain the love perspective listed here in this verse. One such regular definition of love is a deep affection felt for another person whom you have a relationship with. This does not even begin to cover the fruit of the Spirit, love. In the Greek, the word love here is agape. This type of love is not a feeling, but a choice. It's the choice to walk in compassion, to sacrifice, and to consider another's needs greater than one's own. And we of our own selves cannot produce it. It is only produced by the Holy Spirit. It's the kind of love mentioned in Philippians 2:3 "…in lowliness of mind let each esteem others better than himself."

As a matter of fact, all of the tough love Scriptures in the Word of God use agape love. Matthew 5:44 instructs, "But I say to you, love your enemies, bless those that curse you, do good to those who hate you, and pray for those who spitefully use you and persecute you," Luke 6:35 says, "But love your enemies, do good, and lend, hoping for nothing in return; and your reward will be great, and you will be sons of the Most High. For He is kind to the unthankful and evil." John 15:13 reads, "Greater love has no one than this, than to lay down one's life for his friends." 1 John 3:10-11 says, "In this the children of God and the children of the devil are manifest: Whoever does not practice righteousness is not of God, nor is he who does not love his brother. For this is the message that you have heard from the beginning, that we should love one another," And in 1 John 5:2-3 which proclaims, "By this we know that we love the children of God, when we love God and keep His commandments. For this is the love of God, that we keep His commandments. And His commandments are not burdensome."

Without the Holy Spirit working the fruit of God love into our lives, we won't be able to walk in that perfect love at all. Sometimes thinking of the love God and Jesus had for us is overwhelming. God looked at us in that love and sent us Jesus, His only Son, to take the penalty for our sin and Jesus looked at us with that love and consented to die for us to save us from the penalty of that sin. Like when Jesus was on the cross of crucifixion in a painful near-death condition, after being severely beaten to a pulp, spit on, and sneered and scoffed at, He was able to look upon those who hated Him and had done this to Him with that God love and ask Father God to forgive them because they didn't know what they were doing. Wow! That's intense.

The closest thing to "out of love", desiring to take the pain of another on my own life, happened when my son was just about a year old. He got this terrible ear infection and high fever. He was suffering from the pain so much that he wouldn't eat or drink anything. He was lethargic and would just lie there moaning because it hurt so badly. It was all he could do. My heart was breaking for him and I was hurt because he was hurting. I cried out asking for his pain to be taken from him and placed on me. I would gladly have taken it to spare him. But this was my baby, not someone who had cruelly abused me. God and Jesus' love for us would be something like that, but to a greater immeasurable degree. God calls for us to walk in that kind of love by the working of His Holy Spirit within us. What is encouraging is in knowing that it is definitely a process that needs to be walked out, not something God expects to happen overnight.

In our times of prayer, we need to pray that God would cause us to see others through His filter of love. There was a time in my marriage where my husband would just infuriate me with his stubbornness and refusal to even consider seeing things the way I did. It was like he was just angry all of the time. I thought he was really being a "Barney Bad Butt". We disagreed on just about everything, and I wasn't happy and didn't like feeling that way. So, I prayed and asked Father God to allow me to see my husband the way He did. The next time we butted heads, I heard the Spirit say to me to look into my husband's eyes. I did and what I saw melted my heart toward him. When I looked into his eyes, they looked like the eyes of a frightened little baby bunny hidden by tall grass, trying to decide what to do as it heard the sounds of a lawn tractor's blades moving closer and closer. Aww! How could I not love a scared little bunny? After that, whenever I sensed tension building between us, I would look into his eyes, see that scared little bunny, and then pray for him. It didn't take very long for our relationship to grow stronger and to become peaceful after that. Thank you, Father!

God's love is the universal love that all of the different languages of the world understand without a word being uttered. It's the action of God's true love that will touch the heart of and bring a grown man down to his knees in tears. Love, the fruit of the Holy Spirit, is so powerful that nonbelievers, agnostics and even atheists can't help but see it when we walk in and administer it to them. God calls for us to show His true selfless love to a world that is essentially baffled about what true love really is. Thank you, Father, for giving us your love and teaching and empowering us by your Holy Spirit, to walk in it!

The next fruit of the Spirit is joy. Romans 14:17 tells us this. "For the kingdom of God is not eating and drinking, but righteousness and peace and joy in the Holy Spirit." This joy is not an emotion like happiness. Happiness is an emotion that is fleeting. When things are going your way, you are naturally happy but when the tide turns and negative situations arise all around you, your happiness flees. The joy of the Holy Spirit is not fleeting or based upon circumstances. It's a constant and is always within you, deep in your heart. It's like oxygen in the depths of a pool of water. When it lies beneath, it always bubbles up to the surface. Like Psalm 30:5 says, "…Weeping may endure for a night, but joy comes in the morning." As an analogy, at the end of a sorrowful day, night falls, and when you are sleeping, calmed down and resting, the burst of oxygen joy, bubbles right up to the surface and is there again at the first light of morning. Thank you, Jesus! So sure, joy may get tamped down a bit, but it will rise up again like an oxygen bubble in water.

No one can steal your fruit of the Spirit, joy. I have heard people say to others, don't let them steal your joy. And I always think to myself, nobody can steal your joy when the Holy Spirit gives it to you. Again, it may get tamped down for a bit, but it always bubbles right back up. Jesus even tells us that no one can steal our joy in John 16:22. "Therefore you now have sorrow; but I will see you again and your heart will rejoice, and your joy no one will take from you." And how can anyone take your joy from you as you walk in the Spirit? It's as Psalm 16:11 states, "…In Your presence is fullness of joy…" See, The Holy Spirit draws us to God and therefore, without the Holy Spirit, no one would seek the Lord in whose presence we experience true joy even in times of hardship as 1 Thessalonians 1:6 testifies of. "And you became followers of us and of the Lord, having received the word in much affliction, with joy of the Holy Spirit."

The Greek word for joy is chara and it is closely related to the word charis which denotes the gift of grace and the favor of God. So, we can say when the Holy Spirit gives us the gift or fruit of joy, it is because of God's grace and the favor that He bestowed upon us. The only other thing we need to do with the fruit of joy is put it into action and share it, although sometimes our joy can be indescribable as 1 Peter 1:8 tells us. "…Though now you do not see Him, yet believing, you rejoice with joy inexpressible and full of glory."

I love to testify of the joy of the Holy Spirit. So many times, I have had others say to me, you have such a bubbly personality, or they ask, how can you be so happy all of the time? I tell them that it is simple. I always look for something positive and good in every situation. I look for the silver lining in every storm cloud, so to speak. It's always there. You just have to seek God's good purpose for it and rejoice in it. I know from experience that every tragic and terrible thing that has ever occurred in my life has always had an excellent outcome for me later on. I can always see God's working and guiding hand in it. I may not immediately know the reason and not discover it until later, but I also know that He is unchanging, the same yesterday, today, and forever, and as a result, is always working good for me. So, I know beyond a shadow of a doubt that there may be sorrow for a day, but joy always comes in the morning! Thank you, Jesus! As far as the world has fallen in this day, it really needs to see our joy fruit and be drawn to the mountain of the Lord through it.

The next fruit of the Spirit listed is peace. And in the world, we live in right now, peace has never been more important and sought after. We have the Covid-19 pandemic causing upheaval in just about every aspect of our lives. Our media outlets are telling us to live in our new normal as well as our governmental leaders trying to take advantage of the times and trying to take away some of our liberties to make our new normal in the midst of it all. I wince when I hear that phrase, "new normal". I don't need a new normal. My normal is living and abiding in Jesus and nothing new or otherwise can or will change that! Hallelujah! And that is a direct result of the fruit of the Spirit, peace.

Continuing on, companies and businesses have been lost due to Covid. There is an ever-present uncertainty whether our job will be gone at any given time. Children, once straight-A students, are now failing classes due to online learning that has resulted in the absence of the present help that was available before, in class, but isn't now. They needed and relied on it to complete their lessons, but due to the lack of that one-on-one, in class help and instruction time, they can't. They are suffering loneliness as they are being kept from their peers and friends. Then there's adults arguing about wearing masks and receiving vaccinations. There is polarized political debate like never before and the unprecedented large corporations taking sides in that political debate causing numerous uproars. You know what? I'm just going to stop right there although I could go on, because the last thing I desire to do is to stir up chaos and I'm sure I've concisely made my point that humanity needs peace now, more than ever before, as it feels as though the hills and mountains of the earth are being torn apart. The people need God and Jesus who are peace. As Isaiah 54:10 says, "For the mountains shall depart and the hills be removed. But my kindness shall not depart from you, nor shall My covenant of peace be removed," says the LORD, "who has mercy on you."

First and foremost, peace fruit is the peace that surpasses all understanding that Paul speaks of in Philippians 4:6-7. "Be anxious for nothing, but in everything by prayer and supplication, with all thanksgiving, let your requests be known to God; and the peace of God, which surpasses all understanding, will guard your hearts and minds through Christ Jesus." This peace is a peace that the worldly mind cannot comprehend. When we are Spirit filled, we have a peace that is plentiful, available in every situation and unlike anything this world or the people of it can ever offer us. Jesus said in John 14:27, "Peace I leave with you, My peace I give to you; not as the world gives do I give to you. Let not your heart be troubled, neither let it be afraid."

So then, the alternative to being filled with the Spirit and His peace is to be filled with anxiety, filled with uncertainty, filled with apprehension, or filled with depression and fear. How much better to let the Spirit perform His work of growing peace fruit in us to the glory of God! We need to follow, cherish, and hold on to Jesus, our Prince of Peace, of whom Micah prophesied. Micah 5:4-5 "And He shall stand and feed His flock in the strength of the LORD, In the majesty of the name of the LORD His God; and they shall abide, for now He shall be great to the ends of the earth; and this One shall be peace."

The next fruit of the Holy Spirit is longsuffering. It means forbearance or patience. Longsuffering is made up of two Greek words meaning "long" and "temper", or in other words means having a long fuse. When an explosive has a long fuse, it doesn't immediately blow up. We as humans have natural emotions and there is nothing wrong with that as God, in whose image we were created, has emotions too. However, how we respond to those emotions matters. Paul teaches us Ephesians 4:26-27 "Be angry, and do not sin": do not let the sun go down on your wrath, nor give place to the devil." James puts it this way in James 1:19-20 "So then, my beloved brethren, let every man be swift to hear, slow to speak, slow to wrath; for the wrath of man does not produce the righteousness of God. Proverbs 15:18 says, "A wrathful man stirs up strife, but he who is slow to anger allays contention." And Proverbs 19:11 puts it this way, "The discretion of a man makes him slow to anger…" Also, Titus 1:7 advises "For a bishop must be blameless, as a steward of God, not self-willed, not quick-tempered…"

See, longsuffering isn't necessarily waiting a long time for something, but rather having patience with people. Colossians 3:12-13 says, "Therefore, as the elect of God, holy and beloved, put on tender mercies, kindness, humility, meekness, longsuffering; bearing with one another, and forgiving one another, if anyone has a complaint against another, even as Christ forgave you, so you also must do." When we are longsuffering, we don't immediately retaliate out of anger and throw a punch or draw a weapon, but rather, we patiently forebear, not aggressively reacting to negative circumstances, situations or conditions.

When we look out at society today, we see that longsuffering is a lost art. Even standing in a line, we see short fuses where just someone looking at another in a way they perceive as negative, will verbally berate another. We can see short fuses while driving in traffic. Road rage has become a deadly thing causing severe injury to others or even death. Short fuses go off and cause traffic explosions in the forms of accidents and freeway shootings. Then there are the short fuses that cause abuse in homes on both spouses and children. We could say that today's society is too face paced, and everyone needs to slow down including ourselves. We need to be examples to others and walk in longsuffering to point them to Jesus. Just as Father God and Jesus are longsuffering with us, so we must be with others.

The next fruit of the Spirit is kindness. The definition of kindness is the quality of being friendly, generous, and considerate. It's goodness in action, sweetness of disposition, gentleness in dealing with others. The best way to describe kindness is to look at the encounters with everyday people Jesus had. He was always serving other people. He healed them of diseases, fed them when they were hungry, forgave them of their trespasses, washed their feet and delivered them from evil spirits. Nobody did anything to deserve all of that, but Jesus, out of the kindness of his heart, did all of those things anyway, freely, and without any hesitation.

As we discussed, people in society have grown shorter and shorter fuses amid all the chaos of the times we are in and therefore need us to have the fruit of the Spirit kindness operating in us toward them. When we do, we reflect the character of God and Jesus to them. Joel 2:13 reads, "So rend your heart, and not your garments; return to the Lord your God, for He is gracious and merciful, slow to anger, and of great kindness; and He relents from doing harm." Also, Jonah 4:2 says, "...for I know that You are a gracious and merciful God, slow to anger, and abundant in loving-kindness, One who relents from doing harm." In both of these passages, we see slow to anger followed by kindness. Both are linked together showing us that when we are longsuffering towards others, we offer them kindness. They go hand in hand. As a matter of fact, when we begin to walk in the fruit of the Spirit love, all of the other fruits line up and follow right behind, sort of like cause and effect. Thank you, Lord!

Goodness is the next fruit of the Spirit that Paul listed. A lot of people consider kindness and goodness to be the same thing, but there is a distinct difference. Kindness is more action based while goodness is something deep down inside, existing in the very core of our makeup when this fruit is made manifest in us. The Greek word for goodness, agathosune, doesn't refer to a mindset or an incentive, but rather a way of life characterized by virtue and generosity. It has a drawing power to it, drawing others to us so that we may point the way to Jesus. It's much like small children having an innate ability to be drawn to kindness in people and pick them out in a crowd when they feel threatened or unsure. Walking in the fruit of goodness has the same effect on adults when they are seeking answers in the midst of worldly chaos.

God alone is good as Jesus said in Mark 10:18, but via the work of the Holy Spirit in us, He replicates His goodness into our hearts, and it shows in our lives. Luke 6:27 teaches, "But I say to you who hear: Love your enemies, do good to those who hate you…" With the fruit of goodness working in us, we still do good to those who have wronged us. For instance, you're standing and waiting in a long line for returns, when a young mom with a small child cuts in front of you explaining they were at one point next in line, but she had to leave because her little child had to use the restroom and now she's facing a time crunch for picking up another child from the bus stop. Instead of demanding they go to the end of the line, you allow them to stay put in front of you. You show them goodness, compassion and understanding.

The goodness fruit is like a carbonated drink. Every time it gets shaken up, it just fizzes up, overflows and gushes out. This Holy Spirit given goodness empowers us to live lives differentiated by the desire to act honorably and for the practical benefit of others over ourselves. It is worked in us by studying the Word of God and having it in our hearts. Romans 12:2 urges us "And do not be conformed to this world, but be transformed by the renewing of your mind, that you may prove what is that good and acceptable and perfect will of God." By doing so, we become equipped for every good work as it teaches us in 2 Timothy 3:16-17 "All Scripture is given by inspiration of God, and is profitable for doctrine, for reproof, for correction, for instruction in righteousness, that the man of God may be complete, thoroughly equipped for every good work. Ephesians 2:10 tells us, "For we are His workmanship, created in Christ Jesus for good works, which God prepared beforehand that we should walk in them." Hallelujah! Thank you, Father, for having prepared us for every good work in Jesus!

Faithfulness is the next fruit of the Holy Spirit listed. It encompasses reliability, steadfastness, loyalty and being unwavering. Faithfulness simply means we are full of faith and our actions and conversations display it. The way we become full of faith is by learning of, experiencing, and thereby believing in the faithfulness of God even when things appear impossible to us. Believing that when He says something will happen, it happens. The Holy Spirit works faithfulness in us as we walk with the Lord.

Many Scriptures testify of the faithfulness of God. Let's look at just a few of them. Psalms 89:8 speaks of God's faithfulness. "O LORD God of hosts, who is mighty like You, O LORD? Your faithfulness also surrounds You." We also have Deuteronomy 7:9. "Therefore know that the LORD your God, He is God, the faithful God who keeps covenant and mercy for a thousand generations with those who love Him and keep His commandments." In the New Testament, we find 2 Thessalonians 3:3. "But the Lord is faithful, who will establish you and guard you from the evil one. 1 Corinthians 10:13 says, "No temptation has overtaken you except such is common to man; but God is faithful, who will not allow you to be tempted beyond what you are able, but with the temptation will also make the way of escape, that you may be able to bear it."

This fruit of faithfulness relates to honesty, trustworthiness and truth and is much needed today in the world we live in. Our society has become faithless as our leaders have shown faithfulness only to themselves. The people have become materialistic and self-centered with goals of getting everything that they can, any way that they can, regardless if that goal causes harm to others. Hardly anybody trusts or has faith in those in authority anymore. Not our police, not our government, not corporations, not pharmaceutical companies and not the media as the newly coined phrase "fake news" testifies of. And sadly, not even in some clergy. But because of this, walking in the fruit of faithfulness will cause us to stand out and cause those around us to take notice as we walk opposite of our modern culture. And as they notice and keep their eyes upon us, we can let our light shine before them and testify of Jesus our oasis. Nothing takes God by surprise, so let's make wise use of the times God has us walking in, by being faithful to Him, our family, friends, co-workers, bosses, and everyone else we have some sort of relationship with, being an example of God and His Son Jesus, the faithful and true one. Amen!

Gentleness, the next fruit of the Spirit, is defined in several different dictionaries as considerate or kindly in attitude; tender. Mild and soft. Carefulness, politeness, mildness of temper, calmness of spirit, and as an unruffled disposition. In Greek it is prautes and is translated as gentleness, consideration, humility, and meekness. The first thing that comes to my mind when I think of gentleness is the way I handled my newborn babies. I picked them up, held them, changed them, dressed them, actually, everything I did with them was with gentleness. This mind imagery made me think of Jesus as the shepherd and the way He handles His sheep. Isaiah 40:11 says, "He will feed His flock like a shepherd; He will gather the lambs with His arm, and carry them in His bosom, and gently lead those who are with young." Here we find He tends the flock gently rather than driving them hard with a whip. He gathers the lambs, the babies, and carries them Himself, in His arms upon His bosom. This shouts of gentleness!

The next thing that came to mind was how Jesus truly felt about Jerusalem although her leaders, the Pharisees and scribes ridiculed him, made false accusations against Him and tried time after time to set traps for Him, yet, His heart bled for them. Matthew 23:37 reads, "O Jerusalem, Jerusalem, the one who kills the prophets and stones those who are sent to her! How often I wanted to gather your children together, as a hen gathers her chicks under her wings, but you were not willing!" I hear Jesus' heart crying out don't let your life end with, "But you were not willing." This ultimately depicts a gentle spirit and teaches there is a time for tough love like the times Jesus spoke the woes to the scribes and Pharisees, but there are also times that just a gentle and loving touch is all that is really needed to handle certain situations.

Jesus showed this gentleness in dealing with others also, like the woman at the well who divorced five husbands and was living with a man who wasn't a husband at all. Also, with the adulterous woman whom by law could be stoned to death. But rather, Jesus dealt gently with her instead, sparing her life and telling her to go and sin no more. Paul recognized this attribute of Jesus and allowed the gentleness fruit of the Spirit to work in his own life. 2 Corinthians 10:1 says, "Now I, Paul, myself am pleading with you by the meekness and gentleness of Christ—who in presence am lowly among you but being present am bold toward you."

Jesus wants us to deal with others in the same way He did as the Holy Spirit empowers us with the fruit of gentleness. We find this in Galatians 6:1. "Brethren, if a man is overtaken in any trespass, you who are spiritual restore such a one in a spirit of gentleness, considering yourself lest you also be tempted." And in 2 Timothy 2:24-25, "And a servant of the Lord must not quarrel but be gentle to all, able to teach, patient, in humility correcting those who are in opposition, if God perhaps will grant them repentance, so that they may know the truth..." And Philippians 4:5 tells us "Let your gentleness be known to all men. The Lord is at hand."

As most of our leaders in today's society have become the equivalent of a brood of vipers, shunning the ways of God, we need to walk in sharp contrast to them. We need to walk in the fruit of the Spirit of gentleness so that people can see it and know that the Kingdom of God is at hand as we offer Jesus the oasis to them as a lifeline in the midst of dry sinking sand! Thank you, Lord, for your Holy Spirit who teaches us, of your ways!

The final fruit of the Holy Spirit is self-control. Self-control naturally leads to perseverance as we value the long-term good instead of the instant gratification of the world, like those who lived in Sodom and Gomorrah. They had no self-control and therefore doomed themselves. 2 Peter 2:6-9 says, "and turning the cities of Sodom and Gomorrah into ashes, condemned them to destruction, making them an example to those who afterward would live ungodly; and delivered righteous Lot, who was oppressed by the filthy conduct of the wicked (for that righteous man, dwelling among them, tormented his righteous soul from day to day by seeing and hearing their lawless deeds) — then the Lord knows how to deliver the godly out of temptations and to reserve the unjust under punishment for the day of judgment," This is an extremely motivating passage of Scripture to allow the Holy Spirit to work with and within us, the fruit of self-control.

Paul wrote about self-control in his letter to Titus, in chapter 2 verses 11-13. It reads, "For the grace of God that brings salvation has appeared to all men, teaching us that, denying ungodliness and worldly lusts (self-control), we should live soberly, righteously, and godly in the present age, looking for the blessed hope and glorious appearing of our great God and Savior Jesus Christ."

In the natural world of sports, contestants engage in self-control in order to compete to win a title or perhaps even a trophy. In wrestling for example, a contestant may need to lose some weight in order to compete in a certain weight class for the next meet. They therefore avoid sweets, fried foods, salty foods and foods of high caloric content, you know, all of the best tasting foods. They instead eat vegetables, lean meats, low fat products, and foods high in fiber and protein. Paul understood this concept of natural self-control and used it as a way to encourage us in our spiritual walk. He writes about it in 1 Corinthians 9:24-27. "Do you not know that those who run a race all run, but one receives the prize? Run in such a way that you may obtain it. And everyone who competes for the prize is temperate in all things. (Practices self-control) Now they do it to obtain a perishable crown, but we for an imperishable crown. Therefore, I run thus: not with uncertainty. Thus, I fight not as one who beats the air. But I discipline my body and bring it into subjection, (practice self-control) lest, when I have preached to others, I myself should become disqualified."

The Scripture that has personally helped me the most in exercising the fruit of self-control in my life when a temptation or foolish thought enters my mind is 2 Corinthians 10:5. It says, "casting down arguments and every high thing that exalts itself against the knowledge of God, bringing every thought into captivity to the obedience of Christ," See, everything we do or engage in, starts with a thought. So, when a stupid thought enters my mind that goes against what I know to be true or right, I cast it down before the thought takes hold of my mind for me to ponder upon and allow that thought to grow and become stronger or take up occupancy in my mind. I'll say something like this, "Shut up! You know doggone well that exalts itself against the knowledge of Christ! I cast you down and command you to get out of my head! I'm not stupid, you know!" And boom! That thought is gone and done with, and I feel good and free.

See, self-control is a fruit that frees us. It frees us to enjoy the benefits of a healthy body. It frees us to rest in the security of good stewardship. It frees us from a guilty conscience from doing something wrong. Self-control restricts the pandering to our foolish desires, and we find the freedom to love and live as we were meant to. Jesus wants us to walk in the Spirit, exhibiting the fruits of the Holy Spirit for the world to see and be drawn to Him.

In contrast, Satan wants us to pander to all that is in the world—the lust of the flesh, the lust of the eyes, and the pride of life in order to draw more people to him. Satan wants to lure us into displaying the works of the flesh mentioned in contrast to the fruit of the Spirit in Galatians 5:19-23 "Now the works of the flesh are evident, which are: adultery, fornication, uncleanness, lewdness, idolatry, sorcery, hatred, contentions, jealousies, outbursts of wrath, selfish ambitions, dissentions, heresies, envy, murders, drunkenness, revelries, and the like…" We can say assuredly that Satan wants humans to love the world and its carnality, especially losing self-control—the thing that stops us from committing the above-mentioned works of the flesh and keeps us demonstrating the fruit of the Spirit. But he's a loser with a capitol "L"!

Yes, we are in a battle, but we are God's children, living in Jesus the oasis and with Jesus the oasis living in us. Be encouraged knowing that neither God nor Jesus have ever lost a battle, and being unchanging, we know they never will, but Satan? He keeps losing battle after battle! He lost when he got himself kicked out of heaven and cursed for all eternity trying to exalt himself above God, he lost when Pharaoh let the Israelites go, he lost when he tried to tempt Jesus in the desert, he lost when he attacked Job, he lost when Joseph refused to lie with Potiphar's wife, he lost when Jesus rose from the dead, he lost when he tempted Peter, he lost when Paul had his Jesus encounter on the Damascus road, and he lost when you said yes to Jesus. He has lost every single time a sinner has repented and turned to Jesus as the Lord of their life and their friend. And he loses every time a fruit of the Spirit is exhibited in you. Hallelujah!

Yes Lord, allow your Holy Spirit to manifest and ripen the fruits of the Spirit within us to keep us winning and keep Satan losing and on the run so that we may say the same thing Jesus did in John 14:30, which is, the devil has no hold on me! This is the power that walking in the fruit of the Holy Spirit brings us! Thank you, Jesus! Amen!

CHAPTER TEN

OUTSIDE THE CITY GATES

Revelation 22:14-15 says, "Blessed are those who do His commandments that they may have the right to the tree of life and may enter through the gates into the city. But outside are the dogs and sorcerers and sexually immoral and murderers and idolaters, and whoever practices a lie."

The opposite of the truth is a lie. What is the truth? Jesus is the truth. Who is Jesus? He's the entire Word of God. Therefore, anything contrary to the Word of God or the Holy Bible is a lie. Who is on the outside of the gates of the heavenly city? Whoever loves and practices a lie. Why? Because the devil is a liar and is the father of them as John 8:44 teaches us. Remember when Jesus spoke to the Pharisees, He said, "You are of your father the devil, and the desires of your father you want to do. He was a murderer from the beginning, and does not stand in the truth, because there is no truth in him. When he speaks a lie, he speaks from his own resources, for he is a liar and the father of it." Again, who is outside the city gates? Whoever loves and practices a lie.

Revelation 22:18-19 warns us of this. "For I testify to everyone who hears the words of this book: If anyone adds to these things, God will add to him the plagues that are written in this book; and if anyone takes away from the words of this book of this prophecy, God shall take away his part from the Book of Life, from the holy city, and from the things which are written in this book." God said the same thing concerning the law He had given to Moses in Deuteronomy 4:2. "You shall not add to the word which I command you, nor take from it, that you may keep the commandments of the LORD your God which I command you." And Proverbs 30:6 says, "Do not add to His words, lest He rebuke you, and you be found a liar." Remember, liars have no place in the holy city, New Jerusalem.

To add to "these things" concerns the expounding, teaching and actions in relation to the Word of God. The actions and systems of the Pharisees and scribes are the best example in the Word, of what this means. They took the pure law of God, corrupted, perverted and enforced it, even to death, for their own gain, by adding their own unwritten traditions and making their own words higher and of more significance than the law itself. In doing so, they breached the law. As discussed in chapter six, they were teaching as doctrines the commandments of men and they therefore took away the key of knowledge from others as a result. And sadly, the corruption and perversion of the law by the Pharisees has been mimicked by many churches, denominations, cults and religions that place men's traditions above the Word of God. By doing so, they are adding to the words within it.

Again, Revelation 22:14 tells us "Blessed are those who do His commandments that they may have the right to the tree of life and may enter through the gates into the city." Revelation 21:8 says, "But the cowardly, unbelieving, abominable, murderers, sexually immoral, sorcerers, idolaters, and all liars shall have their part in the lake of fire and brimstone, which is the second death." And Revelation 21:27 warns us, "But there shall by no means enter it anything that defiles, or causes an abomination or a lie, but only those who are written in the Lamb's Book of Life."

Now let's go back through the Word and look at some Scripture about lies with the understanding that all in all, no liars are allowed into the eternal kingdom of God, but rather will be thrown into the eternal lake of fire. We'll start in the Book of Proverbs. Proverbs 6:16-19 has a list of the things God hates and lies are listed. It says, "These six things the LORD hates, yes, seven are an abomination to Him: A proud look, a lying tongue, hands that shed innocent blood, a heart that devises wicked plans, feet that are swift in running to evil, a false witness who speaks lies and one who sows discord among brethren."

Proverbs 12:17-22 teaches, "He who speaks truth declares righteousness, but a false witness, deceit. There is one who speaks like the piercings of a sword, but the tongue of the wise promotes health. The truthful lip shall be established forever, but a lying tongue is but for a moment. Deceit is in the heart of those who devise evil, but counselors of peace have joy. No grave trouble will overtake the righteous, but the wicked shall be filled with evil. Lying lips are an abomination to the LORD, but those who deal truthfully are His delight."

Proverbs 14:5 "A faithful witness does not lie, but a false witness will utter lies." Proverbs 21:6 "Getting treasures by a lying tongue is the fleeting fantasy of those who seek death." Proverbs 17:4 "An evil doer gives heed to false lips; a liar listens eagerly to a spiteful tongue." Proverbs 19:9 "A false witness will not go unpunished, and he who speaks lies shall perish." Proverbs 26:28 "A lying tongue hates those who are crushed by it, and a flattering mouth works ruin."

And in Psalm 63:11, we find, "But the king shall rejoice in God; everyone who swears by Him shall glory; but the mouth of those who speak lies shall be stopped." As well as Psalm 31:18 "Let the lying lips be put to silence, which speak insolent things proudly and contemptuously against the righteous." Also Psalm 101:7 "He who works deceit shall not dwell within my house; he who tells lies shall not continue in my presence." This last Scripture here sounds exactly like Revelation 22:15 that we discussed at the beginning of this chapter in stating that no liars shall dwell within the city gates.

Now as far as taking away from the Word of God, when any one person, or group of people say that any part of the Word was for only back then, but not for now, are dismissing a portion of the Word of God. Whether it is in saying the Old Testament isn't relevant for today or that the power, gifts, miracles and moving of the Holy Spirit were for the early church only to establish it, but aren't meant for today, or that they aren't meant for this season and hour of God, are taking away from His Word. But the whole Word of God is truth, the whole truth, and nothing but the truth. And as we learned earlier, Jesus mirages are taking away from the Word in only choosing the best parts of it, pandering to the flesh man, and leaving out the parts that are more difficult and bring us to maturity in Him.

Back in Genesis 3:1, the Bible told us that the serpent, that devil of old, was the most cunning, crafty, subtle, and shrewd of all of the wild animals or beasts that God had created. This signifies that he is a deceitful liar and very good at it. He tells subtle lies by being sneaky, devious, clever, and prudent, operating in trickery. He operates this trickery via the weakest part of man, which is the flesh man, the carnal man, the make it all about "ME" part of us. And as previously discussed, he makes his maneuvers through the lust of the flesh, lust of the eyes, and the pride of life. In understanding this, we see how he then, is the head of the spirit of antichrist. The obvious spirit of antichrist declares that there is no God. And if one believes there is no God, they obviously don't believe that Jesus is the Son of God. Also, Ephesians 6:12 says, "For we do not wrestle against flesh and blood, but against principalities, against powers, against the rulers of the darkness of this age, against spiritual hosts of wickedness in the heavenly places."

While I was studying the Scriptures about lies and liars for this chapter, the Holy Spirit showed me a strategy of the enemy that is ongoing and growing exponentially in today's culture. He showed me that although the devil's ultimate goal is to have mankind believe there is no God and therefore no Jesus, the "spirit of the antichrist" is too blatantly obvious to those who do believe that Jesus is the Son of God. So, in his cunningness, he devised a plan to infiltrate the body of believers with subtle, sly deceptions, preying on those whom he perceived as the weakest, not yet perfected, carnal believers, the immature and yet babes in Christ. How? With partial Jesuses, Jesus mirages!

Remember, we learned that Jesus mirages were formed by the bending and twisting of the light and truth (Jesus), through a layer of hot air or lies and nonsense, close to the desert floor or dry places void of water, the Holy Spirit. And Jesus said in Matthew 24:24-26 "For false christs and false prophets will arise and show great signs and wonders to deceive, if possible, even the elect. See, I have told you beforehand. Therefore, if they say to you, 'Look, He is in the desert!' do not go out…"

The enemy is layering the truth with subtle lies and deception and some leaders have accepted them and therefore are following and teaching the lies wrapped in truth. And so consequently, their followers of that teaching are believing the lies as well. The devil is catering to the flesh part of man by teaching some truths of the Word mingled among lies and untruths and falsehoods, hoping we will believe those lies since they are all mixed in with the truth. He is catering to our weak flesh, slipping in some lies swathed in truth hoping those lies go undetected, thereby robbing many from entering the kingdom of God, the Holy City.

We must do as Romans 12:2 instructs us to. "And do not be conformed to this world, but be transformed by the renewing of your mind, that you may prove what is that good and acceptable and perfect will of God." And 2 Timothy 2:15 "Be diligent to present yourself approved to God, a worker who does not need to be ashamed, rightly dividing the word of truth." Acts 17:11 reads, "These were more fair-minded…in that they received the word with all readiness and searched the Scriptures **daily** to find out whether these things were so." And that is exactly what we need to be doing, as well as why Jesus said, as He taught how to pray in Matthew 6, "Give us this day our **daily** bread." We need to walk with Jesus **daily**.

Hebrews 5:14 teaches us, "But solid food belongs to those who are full of age, that is, those who by reason of use have their senses exercised to discern both good and evil." 1 Thessalonians 5:19-22 says, "Do not quench the Spirit. Do not despise prophesies. Test all things; hold fast what is good." We should do these things earnestly as we recognize what the spirit of the age is up to. We need constant awareness and discernment so that we don't get deceived by or attracted to Satan's false but compelling promises that he carefully crafts according to our weaknesses.

While praying and seeking the Lord in what He wanted me to present in this chapter, the Holy Spirit led me turn to Daniel 7:25 which says, "He shall speak pompous words against the Most High, Shall persecute the saints of the Most High, And shall intend to change times and law…" Here persecute means to weary, wear out, or harass, just as Lot was wearied in Sodom and Gomorrah. The word "times" means appointed occasions or seasons, and "law" refers to a royal edict, statute or commandment. We can look out in our culture today and see the intentions of the spirit of the age. Christians are being harassed with the changing of laws by our leaders and the changing of God's royal edicts or commandments, and by those whom the changes benefit. As an example, God's seventh commandment is "You shall not murder", but our lawmaking abortion legal adds to His Word and changes His commandment to, you shall not murder unless you have an unwanted pregnancy, then you can murder if that life is still in the womb.

Or the changing of the statutes of God like in Genesis 2:24 "Therefore a man shall leave his father and mother and be joined to his wife, and the two shall become one flesh." And Leviticus 18:22, "And you shall not lie with a male as with a woman. It is an abomination." Also, Corinthians 6:9-10 reads, "Do you not know that the unrighteous shall not inherit the kingdom of God? Do not be deceived. Neither fornicators, nor idolaters, no adulterers, nor homosexuals, nor sodomites…will inherit the kingdom of God." But some of our laws have been changed and have made same sex marriage legal and other laws catering to the LGBTQ sect. This is so heartbreaking because they are paving a path to hell for these people if they don't come to the truth, repent, and change their ways.

These changed man made laws certainly try to change God's royal edicts and statutes and are for the purpose of the enemy attempting to change the appointed occasion or season of God. The Scriptures tell us that Jesus is coming back for His bride without spot or wrinkle or any such thing. And it is plain that the intention of the spirit of the age is deceiving the people and leaders by the changing of laws, in an attempt to alter the appointed season or occasion of Jesus' return. But we know it is God who changes the times and seasons as Daniel 2:21 tells us. "And He changes the times and the seasons; He removes kings and raises up kings; He gives wisdom to the wise And knowledge to those who have understanding." And we also know the marriage of the Lamb is indeed coming! Nothing the devil does will stop it! Thank you, Father!

In reading the words in Revelation 22:15, "whoever practices a lie", we should recognize that practicing a lie refers to more than just speaking a lie. We most certainly shouldn't lie as Colossians 3:9 states "Do not lie to one another, since you have put off the old man with his deeds". But rather, practicing a lie indicates moving in, or acting within a realm of lies. It goes deeper than telling a lie. It signifies living in a spirit of a lie or lies and is the "practicing a lie" we are talking about here.

Romans 1:24-32 tells us why it is so important to not "practice lies". It reads, "Therefore God also gave them up to uncleanness, in the lusts of their hearts, to dishonor their bodies among themselves, who exchanged the truth of God for the lie, and worshipped and served the creature rather than the Creator, who is blessed forever. Amen. For this reason, God gave them up to vile passions. For even their woman exchanged the natural use for what is against nature. Likewise, also the men, leaving the natural use of a woman, burned in their lust for one another, men with men committing what is shameful, and receiving in themselves the penalty of their error which was due. And even as they did not like to retain God in their knowledge, God gave them over to a debased mind, to do those things which are not fitting; being filled with all unrighteousness, sexual immorality, wickedness, covetousness, maliciousness; full of envy, murder, strife, deceit evil-mindedness, they are whisperers, backbiters, haters of God, violent, proud, boasters, inventors of evil things, disobedient to parents, undiscerning, untrustworthy, unloving, unforgiving, unmerciful; who, knowing the righteous judgment of God, that those who practice such things are deserving of death, not only do the same but also approve of those who practice them."

God's turning them over to a debase or reprobate mind indicates, most certainly, that there is a time when His grace and mercy can and will run out. So much for the carnal Jesus and the all grace and mercy Jesus mirages.

We should also note that because the devil is so cunning and sly, he also tries to deceive us into believing we are at war with other people due to opposing mindsets and beliefs rather than the spiritual warring spoken of in Ephesians 6:12. He wants us to believe we should war with other flesh, that it is flesh against flesh and not flesh against "spiritual wickedness" as the Scripture teaches us. The devil tries this because as long as he can cause that lie and deception to be alive in the minds of men, then we can't walk in love for others. If we see others as the enemy and therefore fight against them, we can't love them as we love ourselves, which is the second greatest commandment Jesus gave to us, followed by the first, to love God with all of our hearts, souls, and minds.

Next, let's look deeper into what the Scripture says about the spirit of antichrist. 1 John 4:1-3 reads, "Beloved, do not believe every spirit, but test the spirits, whether they are of God, because many false prophets have gone out into the world. By this you know the Spirit of God: Every spirit that confesses that Jesus Christ has come in the flesh is of God, and every spirit that does not confess that Jesus Christ has come in the flesh is not of God. And this is the spirit of the Antichrist, which you have heard was coming, and is now already in the world."

I hear the Spirit saying, it's not necessarily only a confession of the tongue, but by actions and deeds as well. It's like the old adage, actions speak louder than words. Remember, Jesus declared in Matthew 15:7-8 "Hypocrites! Well did Isaiah prophesy about you saying: "This people honors Me with their lips, But their heart is far from Me." The Pharisees confessed God with their tongue, but their actions showed something different. This is why Jesus told us that we would know them by their fruits. Also, Paul in Titus 1:16 taught, "They profess to know God, but in works they deny Him, being abominable, disobedient, and disqualified for every good work."

1 John 2:21-23 says, I have not written to you because you do not know the truth, but because you know it, and that no lie is of the truth. Who is a liar but he who denies that Jesus is the Christ? He is antichrist who denies the Father and the Son. Whoever denies the Son does not have the Father either; he who acknowledges the Son has the Father also."

1 John 1:6 says, "If we say that we have fellowship with Him, and walk in darkness, we lie and do not practice truth." 2 John 1:7 reads "For many deceivers have gone out into the world who do not confess Jesus Christ as coming in the flesh. This is a deceiver and an antichrist." 1 John 3:2-8 states "Whoever commits sin also commits lawlessness, and sin is lawlessness. And you know that He was manifested to take away our sins, and in Him there is no sin. Whoever abides in Him does not sin. Whoever sins has neither seen Him nor known Him. Little children, let no one deceive you. He who practices righteousness is righteous, just as He is righteous. He who sins is of the devil, for the devil has sinned from the beginning. For this purpose the Son of God was manifested, that He might destroy the works of the devil."

Satan is at work twisting good things into harmful ones by bending what is appropriate in the eyes of God, creating Jesus mirages, but this should not take us by surprise. 1 Tim 4:1-2 tells us of this. "Now the Spirit expressly says that in the latter times some will depart from the faith, giving heed to deceiving spirits and doctrines of demons, speaking lies in hypocrisy…"

2 Thessalonians 2:7-12 says, "For the mystery of lawlessness is already at work; only He who now restrains will do so until He is taken out of the way. And then the lawless one will be revealed whom the Lord will consume with the breath of his mouth and destroy with the brightness of His coming. The coming of the lawless one is according to the working of Satan, with all power, signs, and lying wonders, and with all unrighteous deception among those who perish, because they did not receive the love of truth, that they might be saved. And for this reason God will send them strong delusion, that they should believe the lie, and that they may be condemned who did not believe the truth but had pleasure in unrighteousness."

Remember, Jesus told us that not everyone who calls Him Lord will enter the kingdom of God despite them believing they were going to be granted entrance. As a matter of fact, Jesus says in Luke 13 that many will seek to enter and will not be able to, and He'll say, "I do not know you, where are you from. Depart from Me all you workers of iniquity." He was letting them know they were from outside the city gates.

After I had finished reading the above Scripture in 2 Thessalonians, verses 7-12, the Lord had me turn to the book of Daniel and read Daniel 8:23-26. It says, "And in the latter time of their kingdom, When the transgressors have reached their fullness, A king shall arise, Having fierce features, Who understands sinister schemes. His power shall be mighty, but not by his own power; He shall destroy fearfully and shall prosper and thrive; He shall destroy the mighty, and also the holy people. Through his cunning He shall cause deceit to prosper under his rule; And he shall exalt himself in his heart. He shall destroy many in their prosperity. He shall even rise against the Prince of princes; But he shall be broken without human means. And the vision of the evenings and mornings which was told is true; Therefore, seal up the vision, For it refers to many days in the future."

I couldn't help but notice similar things in both the 2 Thessalonians and Daniel Scriptures and note things that the Lord had revealed earlier, throughout the chapters of this book. These particular things jumped out at me, "latter time", "sinister schemes", "through his cunning he shall cause deceit to prosper under his rule", and "He shall destroy many in their prosperity." There are other portions of this Scripture that resound with me, but these that I have pointed out are things we've previously discussed. And now, the best of all, "He shall even rise against the Prince of princes; But he shall be broken without human means." Hallelujah! Our God is a mighty God! Thank you, Jesus, Lord of lords, King of kings and Prince of princes! Isaiah 54:17 says, "No weapon formed against you shall prosper, And every tongue which rises against you in judgment You shall condemn. This is the heritage of the servants of the LORD, And their righteousness is from Me." Jesus said in Matthew 6:19," …I will build my church, and the gates of Hades shall not prevail against it."

In moving on, the list of the others with negative attributes that are outside the city gates in the opening Revelation Scripture of this chapter, sandwiched between the dogs and those who practice a lie, are pretty self-explanatory. But the Lord wants me to discuss the dogs. Because in our present time, dogs are beloved and referred to as our fur babies, certainly a part of the family. But not in the days the Scriptures were inspired by God and written. Back then, dogs were filthy wild animals, considered unclean things. They wandered around in packs and ate garbage and decomposing flesh. For example, 1 Kings 14:11 "The dogs shall eat whoever belongs to Jeroboam and dies in the city…" Jeroboam was an evil king having done more evil than any king before him and God was pronouncing judgment on him as well as those of his household. Here we learn dogs are carnivorous, feeding on the flesh of men. Remember, our flesh man is the weakest part of us.

1 Kings 21:19, "You shall speak to him, saying, 'Thus says the LORD: "Have you murdered and also taken possession?"' And you shall speak to him, saying, 'Thus says the LORD: "In the place where dogs licked the blood of Naboth, dogs shall lick your blood, even yours."'" Here, God is condemning Ahab for setting up Naboth for murder so that Ahab could take possession of, in other words, to steal Naboth's land. So here we find that dogs drink the blood of men, men who are outside the city gates.

2 Samuel 9:8, Then He bowed himself and said, "What is your servant, that you should look upon such a dead dog as I?" Here, David was showing kindness to his best friend's son who thought of himself as worthless. We find here that dogs represent worthlessness.

Psalms 22:16, "For dogs have surrounded Me; the congregation of the wicked has enclosed Me. They pierced My hands and My feet." Psalms 22:20 "Deliver Me from the sword, My precious life from the power of the dog." Here David is prophesying of the suffering of Jesus while dying on the cross. And here we learn that the dog is the devil, that serpent of old, and that dogs are of the devil and are wicked and dangerous.

Proverbs 26:11 says, "As a dog returns to his own vomit, so a fool repeats his folly." 2 Peter 2:22 reads, "But it has happened to them according to the true proverb: A dog returns to his own vomit…" Here, Peter is teaching about false teachers who had been born again, but then returned to their first state of sinning. We learn that dogs are fools and unclean, and that false teachers are dogs.

Philippians 3:2 reads "Beware of dogs, beware of evil workers, beware of mutilation!" And Isaiah 56:11 says, "Yes, they are greedy dogs which never have enough. And they are shepherds who cannot understand; they all look to their own way, every one for his own gain, from his own territory." Once again, we find false leaders being described as dogs.

In sharp contrast to lies and liars, we have Father God who cannot lie. Numbers 23:19 assures us of this, "God is not a man, that He should lie, Nor a son of man, that He should repent. Has He said, and will He not do? Or has He spoken, and will He not make it good?" And Titus 1:2 states, "in hope of eternal life which God, who cannot lie, promised before time began," as well as Hebrews 6:18-19 which says, "that by two immutable things, in which it is impossible for God to lie, we might have strong consolation, who have fled for refuge to lay hold of the hope set before us. This hope we have as an anchor of the soul, both sure and steadfast, and which enters the Presence behind the veil," And we also have Jesus, the truth! Hallelujah!

Satan ever lives to sow discord among the brethren because he knows when we all come to the unity of the body of Christ, his time is up, and the lake of fire reserved for him will become his eternal home. But in the devil's hatred for mankind, he is blinded in realizing that nothing takes God by surprise, God knows all of these things and has made provisions for all of it. He has set the season, the date and time that no one but He Himself knows. The gates of hell will not prevail against the church, no weapon formed against us shall prosper and nothing the spirit of antichrist does will stop the fulfillment of God's Word! Hallelujah! Thank you, Father!

As I was praying, The Holy Spirit asked me to turn to 2 Corinthians 3:2-3 to show me why all of what He revealed throughout this book was so important. It reads, "You are our epistle written in our hearts, known and read by all men; clearly you are an epistle of Christ, ministered by us, written not with ink but by the Spirit of the living God, not on tablets of stone, but on tablets of flesh, that is, of the heart." I heard the Spirit say that we all are living epistles, meaning letters, and by so being, we are Jesus' living letters of authenticity that the people of the world read. Wow!

A letter of authenticity is a letter that accompanies something of high value which certifies its authenticity. The meaning of authenticity is worthy of acceptance or belief as conforming to, or based on fact, conforming to an original so as to reproduce essential features, not false or imitation features: real, actual, and is genuine and veritable. Veritable shares the sense of actuality and lacks of falsehood or misrepresentation. Authenticity carries the connotation of authoritative confirmation that things or people are what they have claimed.

This is why God is calling for unity among the whole body of Christ and is calling for maturity in this season and walking in the fruit of the Spirit where the devil cannot have any type of hold on us. Jesus is the head and each and every member must reflect that by operating in agreement and harmony with Him. Otherwise, His letters of authenticity are all saying something different. Partial Jesus followers or Jesus mirage followers' letters all read differently. This causes the perceived value of Jesus to drop in the world's estimation of Him. In other words, it devalues our authentic Jesus or worse yet, causes His authenticity to be completely overwritten and obsolete before the world.

This just breaks my heart! This is the reason that God was so hard on Aaron's sons and the priests in Malachi's time and every false prophet and false leader throughout the Word of God, and why Jesus was hard on the Pharisees and scribes. They were all subverting, illegitimating, sabotaging, and undermining either Jesus to come, or Jesus who came and will be coming again. This also is why it is so critically important to follow Jesus the oasis and not any Jesus mirages.

I know a lot of what has been revealed in this book is hard, but it is the tough love that we need in order to come to maturity. As a matter of fact, that is exactly what I told Jesus when He was giving me some of the concepts for this book. I said, "But Jesus, some of those truths are so hard! How can I introduce these hard things and yet compel the readers to desire more of you?" In the next chapter, I will share with you what He answered me with.

CHAPTER ELEVEN

INTRODUCE THEM TO ME

As I alluded to at the close of the last chapter, when Jesus was showing me what He wanted me to write about, I knew there were some Scriptures and truths that were hard, that not everything was smooth and easy, and walking with Jesus wasn't always a pleasant sunny walk through the park or skipping through it while holding balloons and ice cream cones. I knew that tribulations would come, that storms would arise and blow, that the testing of one's faith would crop up, and that there would be fiery trials to go through as He worked in our lives to bring us to maturity in Him. So I then asked Him, "How can I introduce these hard things and yet compel the readers to desire more of you?"

He answered me with, "Introduce them to Me!"

I knew by the way He spoke and put emphasis on the word "Me", that He wanted me to share with you "my" Jesus and our personal walk together. So, I am going to do as He has asked, and introduce you to my Jesus and how sweet and loving and caring He is. I am here to attest to the fact that it doesn't matter what the world may throw at you, with Jesus by your side the whole way, it is all worth it. You don't have to go through anything alone, Jesus is always there beside you, before you, and behind you to comfort, love, protect, prepare, warn and encourage you, and to lead you, hand in hand. He's the sugar that helps the medicine go down, so to speak.

The best way I can think of to describe it is like a woman who has gone through childbirth the very first time. The pain is almost unbearable at times, so much so, that perhaps during labor she determines she'll never have another baby. She may vow, never again! But then, her baby is tenderly placed in her arms and as she gazes at the new little life so innocent and pure, the memory of the painful labor flees; it was just as a vapor. Love arises within her heart, a love different than all others she has ever experienced before. The reward for her labor is priceless and so much greater than anything she could have ever imagined. In other words, it hurt so good.

This is the equivalent of a life walked out in Jesus, however, even more precious than that by ten xillion, quintrillion, jesillion percent. Yes, I just made up a new number. Why? Because Scripture tells us that eye has not seen, nor ear heard, nor have entered into the heart of man the things which God has prepared for those who love Him. In other words, it's completely immeasurable!

I totally understood when the Holy Spirit gave me the revelation of all Christians being the living letters of authenticity of Jesus that the whole world reads, and how those letters can devalue Jesus in another's estimation of Him. It thoroughly resounded with me because there was a time in my life when I cringed at the name of Jesus, that is, until I met Him face to face in my bedroom the night I was at the end of my self-rope. I wrote about it in detail in my last book, Forgiven And Not Forgotten.

Anyway, in getting back to this account, I was a teenage passenger in a car and as the driver and I were cruising down a local highway, I saw a sign way up high, nailed on a telephone pole. It was a piece of wood painted white and had red painted letters that spelled out Jesus. I actually cringed when I read His name. You see, some people in my life and others still in the church I grew up in all shared that they were Christians, living for Jesus, but once I was old enough to start seeing and understanding things differently than before, the way they acted was a complete turn off to me and I did not want to be like them in any way, shape, or form. The experiences I had with them were negative to say the least, and therefore, that Jesus sign repelled me from Him rather than compelled me to Him. So, I had no desire to have anything to do with Jesus after seeing what kind of people did.

But I thank God that He allowed me to try and live my life my way, without Jesus, because in doing so, I did get to the end of myself and cried out to God whom I had loved as a little child. And in answer to my prayer, He sent me Jesus! I personally met Jesus that night in my bedroom and from that point forward have loved Him and continued my personal relationship with Him. And He has held my hand as I walked with Him, and He even carried me when my own strength was weak. But in my weakness, He taught me how strong and powerful and yet gentle and loving He truly is. Thank you, Jesus! He has shown me that He is my refuge, my protector, my defender, my safe harbor, my peace, the soother of my troubled soul, my port in every storm, my way maker, my shoulder to cry on, my joy, and so much more!

After Jesus met me that night in my room, I desired to go to church and went back to the church I had grown up in. After I was baptized in both water and Spirit, God began to bring out the gifting He had placed within me, and I guess some of the church leaders didn't like it. It came back to me that they were saying some horrible things about me including I wasn't being led by God, but by the enemy. They actually said that I was a child of the devil and not of God. This hurt me deeply and I felt rejected. I was flip-flopping back and forth as to whether I believed them or not. I was at home crying about it when Jesus came to me.

He said to me, "Don't be disheartened. It isn't you they don't like; it is Me within you. I understand how you are hurting because My people rejected Me too. Remember when you read that I taught My disciples that if the world hates them, they should know it hated Me before them and that I reminded them that a servant isn't greater than his master so if they persecute Me, they will be persecuted too? And if they accused Me of being of Beelzebub, they would accuse my followers also? And how I explained that the reason for the hatred was because My spoken words revealed their sin and so they then had no excuse for their sin?"

I answered Jesus that I did, and He comforted me once again saying, "It is the same thing here and now. You know that you are Mine. Take heart in that, and in that you know I love you!"

That's my Jesus! He comforted and encouraged me at a time when I desperately needed Him to, and His words gave me the encouragement to continue on in Him and my church. As time went on, more of the same continued and my husband and I knew it was time to leave that church and find another. So, we did find another church where we learned and were trained even more and were actually encouraged to move in our God-given gifts. The pastor took us under his wing and began to pour into us. He even referred to us with terms of endearment and called my husband son, and me, Sissy. He later asked us if we would be interested in holding prayer services in our home on Friday nights, which we did, and the Spirit of God was moving mightily. But again, there came a time when the honeymoon was apparently over.

The pastor told the congregation while he was praying, that God told him that He wanted Pastor to put up cork board all along the south wall of the church and it would be a place where the people would write out their prayer requests and pin them to the wall. Then before every service, we were to all lay hands on the wall, and pray over those requests. We did and testimonies of answered prayer came rolling in.

In the meantime, an older couple came to the church, and Pastor introduced them to my husband and me as old members that had retired and had been traveling for years, but now were home again. After a while, something just wasn't sitting right with us. Every time the woman gave a message in tongues, it was the same exact thing and only consisted of the sounds of, "Come-a-see, come-a-see, come-a-see", over and over again. And every time she gave the message, our pastor was the only one who had the interpretation of the message rather than others who had the gift of interpretation. Even the small children would run around after service repeating "come-a-see" over and over again and laughing. Shortly after that, Pastor said, in the middle of one of his sermons, that we should exercise the gift of tongues so that the Holy Spirit could give us more words. It had apparently gotten his attention somehow or another.

Fast forward about a month, on a Sunday morning...The Holy Spirit moved upon me to give a word of the Lord, and so I obeyed and spoke. I don't remember it word per word, but the gist of it was that the Lord was well pleased with the obedience to His instruction to put up the prayer wall. He was indeed hearing the prayers, listening to the cries of His people, and moving on their behalf. He said to continue being faithful in the things of God and watch and see what blessings He would bestow upon the church as He rewarded the obedience and to expect even greater things given in good measure, pressed down, shaken together and overflowing as He rewarded faithfulness to Him.

That Sunday evening, during service, the same lady gave her same message and Pastor in turn, gave the interpretation, and again, I don't remember the exact words, but it was a harsh word concerning unfaithfulness in finances, and how God is an all-powerful God to be feared and man should not rob God. Upon hearing it, my spirit was grieved, and I had a sense of foreboding. I just sensed something was very wrong and had a sick feeling in the pit of my stomach, an apprehension, however, had no clue as to why. That evening after I had retired for the night, I began my evening prayers and fell asleep praying in the Spirit.

The next day, our pastor called and asked if he could come over and speak with my husband and me that evening. Of course, we agreed. After the children were tucked in for the night, Pastor got a chair from the dining room table and placed it in front of us in the living room as we sat on the couch. He started out by saying he had come to correct me as I was in error. I was shocked and asked him how. He gave reference to the word I had spoken in Sunday morning service and the one he had interpreted in the evening service. He said they were opposites, so I was in error and out of order. It hit me like a hard blow to the stomach, but before I could even think of anything to say, I sensed the presence of the Lord surround me and my heartbeat began slowing down back to a normal rhythm.

Pastor said that the Word tells us God is not double tongued as He cannot lie, so for me to say God is pleased in the morning while God said He wasn't pleased in the evening means I made God be double tongued. Right then, I heard Jesus tell me to use a natural instance where a father is pleased with a son for one thing, but angry at him for another. I heard Him say for me not to be afraid and that He would give me the words to speak. My heart sped back up because I have never ever told a pastor he was mistaken before in my entire life! I was raised to respect my elders and never talk back. And I did not like confrontation at all and would always think of something funny to say to ease any palpable tension in any room, always. This was so contrary to who I was, I always avoided confrontations or arguments, would never defend myself and just would go home or to my room and have a good cry, then get up and carry on. But I did not want to disobey my Lord, so I did as He asked.

I politely and sweetly said, "Pastor, with all due respect, those words were concerning two different things, not the same thing. God can be pleased for one thing and be displeased at another. For instance, a son comes home from school with his report card showing straight A's. He had been getting C's and D's and his father told him he needed to bring his grades up. When the father comes home from work and finds the report card sitting on the table, he is very pleased with his son. The father then heads toward his son's room to praise him. There, he finds his son's room a disaster area and he is angry. He had told his son he had better have his room picked up and tidy by the time he got home from work. The father is not only displeased at the mess, but angry about his son's disobedience. The father is pleased about the grades but at the same time, angry about the dirty room. These are two completely different "arenas."

My pastor replied saying that he was sorry, but the Word says that bitter and sweet water should not flow from the same fountain. I was surprised that he replied with that, and I didn't know what to say next. Then I heard Jesus say, "Ask him about when I speak to the seven churches in the Book of Revelation."

I didn't even think twice about it and responded with the following. "Well, what about in the Book of Revelation when Jesus speaks to the seven churches? Doesn't He say, I know this, this, and this about you, all good things, but follow that up with, but I have this against you?"

I have never seen a person's eyes grow so big and so fast before. I knew he had heard and recognized the Holy Spirit. He then admitted that was indeed correct and apologized, then got up to leave saying he would see us at Wednesday night service. Wednesday night rolled around and as my husband and I walked into church, we were hit with what I can best describe as a cold spiritual brick wall. No one would even look at us let alone speak to us, whereas before, they always greeted us. It was so uncomfortable there that entire evening, that we actually couldn't wait for service to be over so we could go home. I lifted the whole situation up to God whom I trusted explicitly, praying in the Spirit.

Now, let's fast forward to Friday afternoon about two hours before our home prayer meeting. I kept getting a funny feeling that no one was going to come. I told my husband that and he said he was feeling the same way. I didn't know what to do except pray and continue to prepare in case someone did come over. About an hour before prayer time was to begin, there was a knock upon the front door. When I opened it, there was the most cute, adorable elderly couple from church there. When I invited them in, they said that they were not there to stay, but the Lord put it upon their hearts to tell us that no one was coming to the prayer meeting. I thanked them and told them that the Spirit had already let us know. Then they continued on, saying that the Lord wanted us to know why.

They then explained that the new couple that came back were very wealthy and that our pastor was controlled by them every time they came back. They said it was a cycle that happened every four to five years. They told us that was all they would say on the matter except they were led by the Lord to let us know, and to know they were not gossipers or backbiters. They then followed that up in stating that the Lord had also led them to leave again and not return this time. They ended by saying again, that God wanted us to know. They then said, "God bless you two, we know you are of the Lord, and we will continue to pray for you. Seek Him and see what He would have you to do." Then, they left.

I cannot praise and thank my Jesus enough! He was right there beside me, defending me against false accusations and filling my mouth with what to say while under verbal attack. I still marvel over that this very day. That's my Jesus! My sweet Jesus was, is, and always will be, my everything!

Next, I'll share how my Jesus prepared me for some events that were about to happen in my everyday life. One, I didn't realize until after the fact and another where He forewarned me in a dream. That's my Jesus!

I had just finished my medical training and obtained my first job. My daughters were still toddlers at the time and since my husband had switched to afternoons to take care of them while I was furthering my education, we only needed a sitter for a couple of hours a day. My neighbor's teenage daughter was taking care of the girls while I worked. It was a rather nice arrangement. Or so I thought.

I had been working at my new job for just a couple of weeks. I noticed all of the girls had taped up little personalized sayings by their windows and I wanted to do the same at mine. So before work one morning, I picked up my box of cards with encouraging messages based on Scripture that I had been given as a gift. I was thumbing through them, and one just jumped out at me. I brought it to work and taped it to my window that morning. It read, "Nothing is going to happen to you today that together you and I can't handle." It was signed Jesus. Since it was a busy office with five doctors, I thought it was very fitting.

My duty for that day was to work closing, gathering all of the checks, cash and credit slips and once I had balanced them all out, to prepare a deposit slip for the office manager to deposit the next day. But I could not make them balance at all. I tried three times and couldn't find the reason why it was off. By this time everyone had left except one medical assistant who was finishing up her charts. I explained to her that I couldn't make the books for today balance and she said she would help me. She also tried several times and couldn't either.

It was now past the time when we should be leaving, so I called home to let my sitter know I would be late and asked her to make a can of spaghetti for the girls for dinner. Then both the medical assistant and I tried to balance the books again and again, but still couldn't figure out the problem. So, she called the girl who had been at the desk beside me for help but was told she was sure she had not made any errors in recording the payments.

The next thing I knew, the office manager had come back to the office saying the other girl had called her and told her the books were not balancing. She added that therefore, I must have messed with them trying to cover up theft and was not fit for the job. She then let me go and told me to collect my things and she would escort me out. When I reached for the card I had taped to the window and read it, "Nothing is going to happen to you today that together, you and I can't handle", I got goose bumps all up and down my arms and neck and sensed Jesus right at my side. I praised and thanked Him all the way home in between sobs and wiping away tears.

When I pulled up in the driveway, I became immediately concerned because the house was dark with no lights on. When I flicked the switch in the kitchen, I saw no dirty dishes in the sink, or empty can of spaghetti in the trash from the girls' dinner. It then hit me that my girls were home alone, and I went flying toward their bedroom. I turned on the light and they were both in bed sleeping, but beside my youngest daughter's mouth was a pile of mostly bone-dry little crackers she had apparently heaved up and the empty box on the floor beside her bed. I was heartbroken and called my husband after I got the girls up and made them some dinner. I explained to him what I had found, and he was livid!

It turns out that our babysitter was having her boyfriend over while sitting and not taking care of the girls and that particular night had not made them dinner but put them to bed, gave them a full box of mini crackers to share for dinner, then left them unattended as she snuck out wither boyfriend. The girls together ate the whole box and then cried themselves to sleep. Bill and I were in agreement that I would no longer work but stay home to raise the children. We understood that the Lord wanted me home to raise a godly seed.

Anyway, the next day, the other medical receptionist called and apologized because she had made the mistake while entering the numbers. That made me feel better in knowing that everyone there knew I hadn't stolen anything, but I now knew I wasn't supposed to be in the work field. I still am in awe at how Jesus knew everything that was going to happen beforehand and therefore, helped me get through. He led me to choose that particular card so I would know He was with me every step of the way! He was working things out for good even though I had to learn the hard way to seek Him and His will for my life before plunging forward with what I thought was best. That's my Jesus!

Another time Jesus prepared me for what was about to come, is another time I had gone back to work after the children were much older. I was receiving unemployment due to the previous office failing financially, so they downsized, and I was laid off. Then after about two months, I was contacted for a job that I had not applied for but was found through the unemployment office. I decided to accept the position. After working there for a bit, I found it wasn't comfortable there at all. The girls were always afraid to talk to one another and always looking over their shoulders. The atmosphere was not pleasant, but I decided to stick it out for a bit to see where it may go once I had been there a tad longer. During lunch break one afternoon, one of the girls, the only one who actually spoke to me personally, told me that they went through a lot of girls at this office but wouldn't say more. She told me that I would find out on my own soon enough.

One morning shortly thereafter, I awoke from sleep after a dream. In the dream, I was being chased through a jungle. I couldn't see who was chasing me through all of the jungle foliage but knew beyond a shadow of a doubt that I was being stalked. I stopped to rest behind a tree to catch my breath and didn't hear any more movement. I peeked out from the tree and looked behind me only to see the one girl I talked to, while holding up a knife, slowly walking toward my tree, and the office manager holding up an ax, slinking along beside her toward me.

When I woke up, I knew I was being betrayed by the one friend I had made at the doctor's office and she was stabbing me in the back and that I was going to be fired soon by the office manager, you know, get the ax. So, I decided I would write a letter of resignation giving my two weeks' notice on my lunch hour, hand it in at the end of the day, and be done with it. I thanked Jesus for showing me what was going on through the dream.

When I arrived at work, the whole atmosphere there was very cold. The whole morning, I kept noticing out of the corner of my eye, the office manager coming to speak to the only friend I had made there. They were whispering and when I looked over, the office manager would just glare at me. This was confirmation to me the dream was indeed a warning from the Lord.

When it was time for lunch, the office manager came to me and let me go, telling me they were an at-will workplace, and she didn't have to tell me why. I was fine with it. I gathered up my things and walked out the door. Then my friend came running up to me apologizing and said the office manager threatened her job if she didn't do as she was told and she really needed her job, being a single mother of two boys. I told her it was fine; I was going to quit anyway and forgave her. On the drive home, I prayed and felt peace as a huge weight was lifted from me.

Once home, I re-applied for unemployment and a few weeks later received a phone call. The lady from the unemployment office told me that my claim was re-opened, and I was also approved for an additional 26 weeks of unemployment once I finished this first claim. She then told me that my office manager fought my unemployment claim, saying I was trying to sabotage their business. The lady told me she instantly knew it was hogwash as who accepts a job while on unemployment just to try to sabotage the very place they were hired on at? She said it just didn't make any sense at all. After I hung up the phone, I started to praise and thank Jesus again for having my back and preparing me for what was coming that day by revealing it to me in a dream.

But that isn't all of it, for it wasn't long after, that the economy crashed, we went into a recession, and jobs were very hard to come by. Later Jesus showed me that if I had put in that letter of resignation and quit, I would not have qualified for another claim or the two additional unemployment benefit extensions I received from the state, and that He had made provision for me and my family. I bawled like a baby after that in realizing how much Jesus cared for me and had everything taken care of beforehand. That's my Jesus!

The above accounts are just a few of the numerous stories I could share with you about my personal relationship with Jesus. There are so many more where He personally has been there for me through the years, but there just isn't room for them all in this chapter. However, I do hope those I did share, encourage you to seek more of Him, have a closer walk with Him, and for you to desire and allow Him to bring you to a greater degree of perfection in Him. Remember, He loves you, you're the apple of His eye, and He has good plans for you. He wants to defend you when you're falsely accused, He wants to bless you and bless those that bless you and He wants to curse those who curse you. He wants to show you great and marvelous things. Will you let Him into your daily life more and more?

I would like to leave off with this Scripture, as it is my heartbeat for you all…

Colossians 3:12-17. "Therefore, as the elect of God, holy and beloved, put on tender mercies, kindness, humility, meekness, longsuffering; bearing with one another, and forgiving one another, if anyone has a complaint against another; even as Christ forgave you, so you also must do. But above all these things put on love, which is the bond of perfection. And let the peace of God rule in your hearts, to which also you were called in one body; and be thankful. Let the word of Christ dwell in you richly in all wisdom, teaching and admonishing one another in psalms and hymns and spiritual songs, singing with grace in your hearts to the Lord. And whatever you do in word or deed, do all in the name of the Lord Jesus, giving thanks to God the Father through Him." Amen!

Other titles from Higher Ground Books & Media:

Raven Transcending Fear by Terri Kozlowski

The Power of Knowing by Jean Walters

Forgiven and Not Forgotten by Terra Kern

Redeeming Gethsemane by Daniel K. Held

The Seedling by Theresa Garee

Through the Sliver of a Frosted Window by Robin Melet

Breaking the Cycle by Willie Deeanjlo White

Healing in God's Power by Yvonne Green

Chronicles of a Spiritual Journey by Stephen Shepherd

The Real Prison Diaries by Judy Frisby

The Words of My Father by Mark Nemetz

The Bottom of This by Tramaine Hannah

Add these titles to your collection today!

http://www.highergroundbooksandmedia.com

Do you have a story to tell?

Higher Ground Books & Media is an independent Christian-based publisher specializing in stories of triumph! Our purpose is to empower, inspire, and educate through the sharing of personal experiences.

Please visit our website for our submission guidelines.

http://www.highergroundbooksandmedia.com

www.ingramcontent.com/pod-product-compliance
Lightning Source LLC
Chambersburg PA
CBHW061947070426
42450CB00007BA/1076